GOD'S CHURCH
FOR TODAY

God's Church for Today is the first in a
four-book series, CHRISTIAN
FAITH FOR TODAY.
Other books in this series

God's Kingdom for Today
God's Word for Today
God's Salvation for Today

Other books by Peter Toon

Jesus Christ Is Lord
God Here and Now
Free to Obey
Evangelical Theology 1833-1856
Development of Doctrine in the Church

GOD'S CHURCH FOR TODAY

PETER TOON

Cornerstone Books
Westchester, Illinois

Cornerstone Books
Westchester, Illinois 60153

God's Church for Today
© Copyright 1980 by Peter Toon
Printed in the United States of America.

Library of Congress Catalog Card Number
80-65330
ISBN 0-89107-183-0

CONTENTS

PREFACE / 7

1 BORN INTO GOD'S KINGDOM / 9

2 THE CHURCH OF GOD / 16

3 LOOKING BACK / 30

4 LOOKING UP / 50

5 LOOKING FORWARD / 65

6 LOOKING AROUND / 78

7 THE CHURCH OF CHRIST / 92

8 CONCLUSION / 99

APPENDIX: The Ordained Ministry / 103

FURTHER READING / 111

PREFACE

I write this book hoping that it will come especially into the hands of those who, having been "born again" by the Holy Spirit, are in search of a clear understanding of the Church of the Lord Jesus Christ. In particular I am thinking of students in North American colleges and universities. Though I am English, I regard the U.S.A. as my second home and I pray that by this book I shall minister in some small way to Americans and Canadians. Discussion questions are provided at the end of each chapter.

The students of Oak Hill College, where I teach, helped me to clarify my ideas by their response to my lectures on the Church, ministry and sacraments. Other friends fed me with stimulating questions and ideas. Especially I wish to thank Isabel Erickson, Jeff Steenson, Jan Dennis, and Peter Gillquist. My wife cast her critical eye over the whole manuscript.

I have made use of the *New International Version* of the Bible for my quotations.

I dedicate this book to the Right Reverend Drexel Gomez, the Anglican Bishop of Barbados, who with his

wife gave my family such warm hospitality at Easter
1979.

Peter Toon
Feast of the Ascension of Jesus Christ
24th May 1979
Oak Hill College, London

1 BORN INTO GOD'S KINGDOM

When you are born, you enter into a human family, which involves a series of relationships—with mother, father, brother(s), sister(s), aunt(s), uncle(s), cousins, etc. A new baby cannot live in isolation; it needs milk, warmth, and protection. When you are born again (or, born from above), you enter into God's kingdom and family, which also involves a series of relationships—with God—Father, Son, and Holy Spirit—and with others who have been born again. A Christian cannot live in isolation; he needs spiritual food, fellowship, and care (discipline).

When you enlist as a recruit in your country's army, you join others in training to be soldiers, in fighting the enemy, and in defending your land. You are placed in a company with other soldiers, for you cannot function alone. Likewise, when you join the Lord's army, you learn to fight against sin and for righteousness. You learn to fight along with other soldiers of Christ.

To be born again or to become a soldier of Christ are two ways of saying that you have submitted to Jesus Christ as Savior and Lord and God has accepted you. To accept him as Savior is to receive the forgiveness of sins and the gift of eternal life; it is also to become a member of the people who have also accepted him, those "saved" people who are called to be "saints" (1 Corinthians 1:2, *RV*). To be his disciple and follow him as Master and Lord is to do his will and adopt his life style; it is also to join others who are his disciples.

In Christian experience there is a horizontal and a vertical dimension. There is the vertical relationship to God the Father, through Christ, by the Holy Spirit; by this I receive my salvation. And there is the horizontal relationship to other believers; the same Spirit who joins me to the Father and the Son joins me to my fellow-Christians.

One of the useful, practical emphases made by the so-called charismatic or Pentecostalist movement (a movement which has affected churches of many denominations) is this emphasis on Christians belonging to one another in the power of the Spirit and in the name of the Lord Jesus. The ethos of Western culture tends to cultivate individualism, and much Christian experience has been affected by this ethos. I mean to say that from the important and indispensable personal relationship with God enjoyed by all believers has developed an individualistic view of the Christian life and calling. This surfaces particularly when believers speak of how they think God has guided them. "The Lord said . . ." or "the Lord revealed . . ." or "the Lord showed . . ." are common expressions. A personal relationship with God is what being born again by the Spirit produces (Romans 8:16). The same Spirit then wishes to lead the new believer into a local church, where he can function as a committed member of the fellowship.

However, the Spirit who wishes to lead every born-again believer into active church membership has what we may reverently describe as a difficult task! There are competing claims made by different denominations, sects, and groups; there are pressures from family, friends, and organizations to go in specific directions. It is difficult for a sensitive person to discern the leading of the Spirit in this complex religious situation. Yet we know that the Spirit leads Christians according to the will of God revealed in the Holy Scriptures, and this must be our starting point. Our task is to read and interpret the teaching of Scripture in humble reliance upon the Holy Spirit as we make use of that wisdom God has given to Christians over the centuries, especially to biblical commentators and theologians.

To help the reader in this task I want to examine the images or pictures of the Church which we find in the New Testament. I suggest that they help us not only to answer the question, "Which church should I join?" but also to answer the further question, "How can we improve the quality of our church?" There are many images of the Church in the New Testament. Here I will only list ten—"one loaf," "a pillar," "a bulwark," "a chosen race," "the new creation," "the people of God," "lambs who rule," "body of Christ," "the elect," and "flock."

In his *Images of the Church in the New Testament* (1960), Paul S. Minear claims to have found no less than ninety-six. Even if he includes some which others would regard as doubtful or questionable, the fact remains that there is a tremendous variety used by the biblical writers. This should highlight for us the richness of the biblical teaching about the Church. Too often we tie ourselves down to one or two images—e.g., the family or the body of Christ. While there usually appear to be good reasons for our limited usage, God surely wants us to hear as much as possible of his portrayal of his Church. So we need to consider and use more images.

My own study of these images or pictures leads me to believe that, in the context of the New Testament, they make one point absolutely clear. It is this. We cannot separate what may be called the nature or essence of the Church from either its historical form or its function in the world. I do not doubt that in theoretical thinking we can make a distinction, and in clarifying issues such a distinction can be useful. However, the evidence of the New Testament is that the true nature of the Church and its form or actual historical presence in the world are inseparable. The early Church was obviously a community empowered by God and possessing the Holy Spirit, but at the same time it was a human community which sinned, made mistakes, and had quarrels (read 1 Corinthians for evidence!). What the apostolic Church was in relation to God the Father, Son, and Holy Spirit cannot be separated practically from its purpose and activity in the Graeco-Roman world.

In other words, we cannot separate it from its historical reality as we may distill salt from salty water; and we cannot practically distinguish its true nature from its visible, empirical existence as we may remove the husk from the kernel of corn. Its divine and human aspects are inextricably joined together, just as in Jesus of Nazareth the eternal Logos is joined to human flesh (John 1). The humanity of the Son of God was a sinless humanity; the Church is a sinful humanity which the Holy Spirit is leading toward sinlessness. As we shall note in the next chapter, Paul called the divided and confused congregation in Corinth "God's building"!

Bearing in mind that the essence and the historical reality of the Church are bound together, I want to present in the following pages a method of recognizing the Church of God today. Using the biblical images, I shall make clear the necessary relation of essence and form and present two main points.

1. The Church (and therefore each true local church) is to be viewed as nothing less than "the Church of God," a society of divine origin, sustenance, and purpose.

2. Each local church should have four basic aspects or modes of function in order truly to exhibit its character as the "Church of God." I shall present these as "looking back," "looking up," "looking forward," and "looking around." The "looking" which I have in mind is the looking which intends to take action on the basis of what is seen, although the action connected with the different directions of looking is not the same. Therefore,

a. Each local church should *look back* to the people of God in the old and new covenants. This means receiving the Holy Scriptures, in which is the record of God's revelation to Israel, in Christ, and through the apostles. It also means looking to the Church through the Christian centuries as that community into which by grace we ourselves have entered.

b. Each local church should *look up* to God; it has a function to look to God for grace and guidance, to worship and adore him, and to do all its activities in his name for his glory.

c. Each local church should *look forward* in hope to the age to come. It functions as a pilgrim people whose true home lies in God's future.

d. Each local church should *look around* to see not

only the needs of its own membership, but also to proclaim the gospel and respond to the needs of the world in which the church is placed.

Now I recognize that these four aspects do overlap—e.g., I cannot look up to God without knowledge of his revelation contained in Scripture. So I have to look backwards in order to look up. Further, I cannot look up to God without also looking forward to the glory of God to be revealed at the end of the age. Finally, I cannot love God as I look up without loving my neighbor by looking around. However, for the purpose of clarity we must consider each one separately.

I hope that this method will not be confusing to my reader. I create a picture of each true Church as a community which is involved in looking in four directions at one and the same time. This is straightforward, I think. Then, to explain what is involved in each of the four activities of looking, I use a collection of pictures (images) taken from the New Testament. So I am explaining one picture by pointing to a further set of pictures. If this is clearly understood, then what follows should not prove to be too difficult.

Since I am presenting the Church as engaged in a fourfold activity, I cannot effectively demonstrate in this presentation the relation of the Church to our Lord and Savior, Jesus Christ. So I do this in a chapter in which I look particularly at the image of the Church as the "body of Christ" and Christ himself as the "Head" and "Lord" of the Church. In a final chapter I attempt to summarize my argument and answer the question, "Which church should I join?"

QUESTIONS FOR DISCUSSION

1. What is the difference between a personal rela-

tionship with the Father through Jesus Christ and an individualistic relationship to him?

2. Why should a new convert take time and care to choose which local church in which to seek membership?

2   THE CHURCH OF GOD

My task in this chapter is to show how the images of the Church point to its essential nature, its God-dimension as we may call it. However, the reader will notice that the same images which highlight the God-dimension also highlight the human-dimension.

A VARIETY OF IMAGES

In one sentence Paul used two images which affirm the divine origin and character of the local church. He told the members of the imperfect and erring Corinthian congregation that they were God's "field" (or "husbandry" or "garden") and God's "building" (or "temple"). Paul was emphasizing the God-ordained unity of the church and condemning the tendency of the members to associate themselves exclusively with one human evangelist or apostle. He saw the work of Apollos and himself as being for the Lord and only for him. So he wrote: "For we are God's fellow workers; you are God's field, God's building" (1 Corinthians 3:9).

God's field

By this image, familiar to readers of the Old Testament (cf. Isaiah 5:1-7) and drawn from farming or horticulture, we are invited to consider a garden or field and the one who cares for it. A farmer or gardener spends time digging the ground, preparing it for seeds, sowing seeds, watering them, removing weeds, and eventually harvesting the crop. Paul was asserting that although one apostle/evangelist planted seed and another watered it, the field belonged to God and the seed and crop were his. The gospel of Jesus Christ was the seed, and the power of the Holy Spirit caused it to grow in human lives so that a community of believers was created. So the Church is God's field, and remains so despite its imperfections.

God's building

From thoughts of sowing seeds and watering them Paul turned to think of laying foundations and building walls. Whether we think of a civic building or the Jerusalem Temple, the meaning of his picture is clear. As the prospective owner of a building employs workmen to construct that which he has planned, so the Lord uses human agents in the conversion of sinners and creation of churches. Yet the work and the end product are his, and his alone. The Church is composed, as it were, of living stones, whose spiritual life is given by Christ through the Holy Spirit. In using this image Paul probably had Psalm 127:1 in mind: "Unless the Lord builds the house, its builders labor in vain."

Continuing his argument that the Corinthian congregation should recognize its true identity and live as those who belong to God the Father, through the Son and by the Holy Spirit, Paul called the members "the temple of God." "Don't you know that you yourselves are God's temple and that God's Spirit lives in you? If anyone destroys God's temple, God will destroy him; for God's temple is sacred, and you are that temple" (1 Corinthians 3:16, 17). As the presence of the Lord was known within the old Temple of Jerusalem, so within the new-covenant people of God, the divine presence was known (Ezekiel 36:27).

If we turn to Ephesians 2:19-22, we find that Paul expanded his thought as he wrote of the place of Gentile believers in the Church of God. Because of the work of Christ upon the cross, Paul said,

You are no longer foreigners and aliens, but fellow citizens with God's people and members of God's household, built on the foundation of the apostles and prophets, with Christ Jesus himself as the chief cornerstone. In him the whole building is joined together and rises to become a holy temple in the Lord. And in him you too are being built together to become a dwelling in which God lives by his Spirit.

Here Paul used three images for the Church—a city, a family, and a building. In connection with the latter he presented Christ as the "chief cornerstone." In ancient architecture the cornerstone was the primary foundation stone which set the bearings for the entire building. From it the builders worked both horizontally and vertically in setting and then checking the walls. Thus, Christ is the basis on which and the standard by which God builds his Church. In union with him and energized by him, believers are built into God's building (cf. 1 Peter 2:4-8).

So we see that Paul affirmed the divine origin of the Church by describing it as God's field and God's building. He also affirmed that the essence and existence in space and time are inseparable. We move on now to notice how three further images are used by Paul and Peter which emphasize that the Church came into existence and remains in existence by the initiative of God.

The apostles firmly held that as God had chosen ancient Israel to be his special people from Moses until Christ, so also he had chosen new Israel, the Church, to be his special people from Christ to the end of the world. The basic difference in the two periods is that the first Israel were physical descendants of Abraham and thus of one race, while the second were of a variety of races and yet all spiritual descendants (sons) of Abraham (Romans 4:16). The choice of ancient Israel by God is clearly expressed in the following passages:

Although the whole earth is mine, you (Israel) will be for me a kingdom of priests and a holy nation.

(Exodus 19:5, 6)

The LORD your God has chosen you out of all peoples on the face of the earth to be his people, his treasured possession.

(Deuteronomy 7:6)

I took you from the ends of the earth, from its farthest corners I called you. I said, "You are my servant"; I have chosen you and not rejected you.

(Isaiah 41:9)

In their use of the images of "Israel" (Galatians 6:16), "a chosen people, a royal priesthood, a holy nation" (1 Peter 2:9), Paul and Peter were claiming that the existence of the Church is due solely to the initiative and sovereign choice of God.

Apart from this variety of images which highlight the truth that the Church is a divine society, there is in the New Testament much historical and doctrinal material which expresses the same basic idea.

HISTORICAL ORIGINS

Let us consider first the beginning of the Church. Here we find that whether we trace it to the early ministry of Jesus or to the Feast of Pentecost after his resurrection, the origin is divine. Jesus of Nazareth, who told fishermen to leave their nets and follow him, was "the Word (which) became flesh" (John 1:14), possessing "the glory of the one and only Son" of the Father. Because of who he was, his activity possessed the divine initiative. Sent by the Father, he surrounded himself with his "little flock" (Luke 12:32) of twelve apostles and a larger group of disciples. And he actually spoke of Peter as an integral part of the new Church (Matthew 16:16ff.).

In Jerusalem on the day of the Feast, the Church sprang into life in an extraordinary way (Acts 2). Filled with the Holy Spirit, the apostles and disciples were able to preach in a variety of languages the good news of salvation in Christ to the Jews who were living in many countries. Peter delivered a powerful sermon; many were convinced by it and by the behavior of the vibrant disciples that Jesus was risen and was truly the Messiah. "Those who accepted his message were baptized and about three thousand were added to their number that day" (Acts 2:41). Certainly this was a day when God was at work; the Holy Spirit filled the hearts of the disciples, gave them the gift of preaching and made them bold, and opened the hearts of their hearers to receive the good news.

At this stage only Jews were members of the Church; it took another initiative from God to cause Gentile believers to become members. Before Cornelius, a Roman centurion, was baptized as a believer, Peter received a vision from God. Its meaning was that it was the will of God that non-Jewish believers in Christ were to become full members of the Christian community (Acts 10). This theme of God's initiative and guidance of the Church can be traced right through the Acts of the Apostles and the letters to the various churches.

DOCTRINE

We turn now to the doctrinal teaching which affirms the divine choice and origin of the Church. And here we must be selective, for there is much material. As the LORD who revealed himself did so as one God in three Persons—Father, Son, and Holy Spirit—we shall briefly note the role of each Person in the formation of the Church.

Both Paul and Peter affirm that the Father planned the existence and membership of the Church before he made the world. In language particularly appropriate to worship, Paul wrote:

Praise be to the God and Father of our Lord Jesus Christ who has blessed us in the heavenly realms with every spiritual blessing in Christ. For he chose us in him before the creation of the world to be holy and blameless in his sight. In love he predestined us to be adopted as his sons through Jesus Christ, in accordance with his pleasure and will—to the praise of his glorious grace which he has freely given us in the One he loves.

(Ephesians 1:3-5)

Here are sublime thoughts, but the theme of divine election and choice is prominent. Paul expressed similar ideas in Romans 8:29, 30. The apostle Peter put the matter briefly when he wrote that we "have been chosen according to the foreknowledge of God the Father" (1 Peter 1:2).

Those whom God elected or whom he knew would receive the gospel of Christ were sinners, having no direct and meaningful spiritual relationship with himself.

An atonement for sin had to be made and they had to be reconciled to the Father. So Jesus Christ, the Incarnate Son, is presented in the New Testament as the One who by his death on the cross made atonement and brought reconciliation. Referring to himself Jesus said, "I am the good shepherd. The good shepherd lays down his life for the sheep" (John 10:11). Addressing the elders of the Ephesian church, Paul told them to "be shepherds of the church of God, which he bought with his own blood" (Acts 20:28). Later, writing to the whole church, he taught that "Christ loved the church and gave himself up for her" (Ephesians 5:25).

The eternal choice of the Father and the redemption of the Son are objective realities; they have to be applied in time and space to individuals who repent of their sins and turn to the Lord. To assist repentant sinners to believe on the Lord Jesus and to guide them into the fullness of the Christian commitment is the work of the Holy Spirit. Paul taught that no one can from their hearts say "Jesus is Lord" unless the Holy Spirit has been and is at work within him (1 Corinthians 12:3). Jesus explained that "no one can come to me unless the Father who sent me draws him" (John 6:44), and later added that the Father sends the Holy Spirit to convict the world of guilt in regard to sin, righteousness, and judgment and lead sinners to faith in Christ (John 16:8-10).

Peter summarized this saving work of the Holy Trinity when he said that we "have been chosen according to the foreknowledge of God the Father, by the sanctifying work of the Spirit, for obedience to Jesus Christ and sprinkling by his blood" (1 Peter 1:2). Significantly he had called the Christian congregations God's "elect" in verse 1. Paul composed the well-known prayer which

Christians often repeat: "May the grace of the Lord Jesus Christ, and the love of God, and the fellowship of the Holy Spirit be with you all" (2 Corinthians 13:14). The Church exists because of the electing love of the Father, the saving grace of the Lord Jesus, and the cohesive fellowship of the Holy Spirit. Not only the origin, but also the life of the Church is centered in God himself.

GOD'S *EKKLESIA*

I have used and will use the word "church" many times and have not as yet explained its meaning. Here I wish to do so, for its meaning adds weight to the basic theme of this chapter. The New Testament word we translate as "church" or "congregation" is *ekklesia.*

Ekklesia was the word used in the city-states of ancient Greece to describe the assembly of all the citizens. Democracy functioned in this assembly as the citizens voted on major issues such as whether to declare war or make a treaty of peace with another state.

When the Old Testament was translated from Hebrew into Greek, just before the time of Christ, the Jewish translators used *ekklesia* to describe the *kahal*— the congregation or the assembly of Israel. In using the word, they left behind the association with political democracy and gave it a new reference, the call of the Lord. *Ekklesia* was the body of people, the assembly of Israel, who had been summoned from their homes to meet with God or to do his bidding (cf. Psalm 26:12; 68:26; Numbers 1:18; Judges 20:2). It was God's chosen people coming to hear him.

The writers of the New Testament used the Greek Old Testament, and so they took over this word to describe the community of the disciples of Jesus Christ. On a few occasions *ekklesia* refers to the total number of Christians on earth—e.g., 1 Corinthians 12:28 and Ephesians 5:25. More often it refers to a local assembly or congregation of Christians—e.g., 1 Corinthians 11:18; 14:19, 23; Galatians 1:2. By far the commonest description in the New Testament is, surprisingly, not the "church of Christ," but rather the "church of God" (e.g., 1 Corinthians 1:2; 2 Corinthians 1:1; 1 Thessalonians 2:14; 1 Timothy 3:5, 15). So the local church is the assembly of people who have been called out of the world to meet with God; they are God's Church. Baptism is God's covenant sign that we belong to him through Christ (Romans 6).

Too often we think of the local parish church as somehow inferior to the larger denominational or organizational grouping. Yet, as far as the New Testament is concerned, the true local church is the authentic reality, just as the local McDonalds or Kentucky Fried is and sells the real thing. Local churches are linked together not merely organizationally but spiritually—having the same Lord, indwelt by the same Spirit, and praying to the same Father in heaven. This link, being spiritual, has reference to past, present, and future time, as we shall see.

FAITH-KNOWLEDGE

To speak of the congregation which meets in a consecrated building in a particular street of a specific small town is to speak in plain, verifiable language. I may go to that place in my car and check whether in fact a group of people do meet for what they claim are Christian purposes. However, to claim that this congregation is *God's* church in this town is to speak the language of faith; it is not verifiable by normal means.

From God's revelation recorded in Scripture I learn of God's saving and reconciling work, of the creation of his saved community, and of its mission for God in the world. I accept this message by faith, even as I receive the Good News of salvation in Christ for me by faith. Believing in the Savior God, I believe in his loving purposes and accept his Church. Then I believe that this congregation of people in this small town is a part of the Church which Jesus Christ purchased with his sacrificial blood, and so I claim that it is God's church. Only a Christian can make this claim in any meaningful way, for only he has that faith in God which allows him to have this confident knowledge of the true nature of this assembly of people.

Many Christians in their Sunday worship express the content of their faith by using the two great creeds of the Church, the Apostles' and Nicene Creeds. After declaring faith in the Father and the Son they state:

I believe in the Holy Spirit, the holy Catholic Church, the communion of saints, the remission of sins, the resurrection of the flesh and eternal life.

We believe in the Holy Spirit, the Lord, the giver of life. . . . We believe in one holy catholic and apostolic Church.

The Apostles' Creed was originally used in Italy by believers who were being baptized and only later was used in daily services of worship. The original Latin wording, which goes back to around A.D. 200, makes clear that while a Christian is to *believe in* the Holy Spirit *(credo in Spiritum sanctum),* he is to *believe* the Church *(credo ecclesiam).* To believe *in* God—Father, Son and Holy Spirit—is to have saving faith in God. To believe the Church is to be a member of the Church, to believe that it came into being by God's will, and that it is a people in whom the Holy Spirit dwells. (Note that in both creeds the statement on the Church follows immediately after that on the Holy Spirit.)

The Nicene Creed was composed by the ecumenical councils of Nicaea (325) and Constantinople (381). The distinction between *believing in* the Holy Spirit and *believing* the Church is not made in the original Greek of this creed, as it is made in the Latin of the Apostles' Creed. However, many theologians have pointed out that in the actual structure of the Nicene Creed the belief in the one, holy, catholic, and apostolic Church is tied inseparably to belief in the Holy Spirit. Thus we believe in the Church only because we believe *in* the Holy Spirit, whom we believe is present in the Church.

In claiming that the essence of the Church—that is, its God-dimension—is not verifiable, I am not suggesting that church members are not to be obedient, loving disciples of Jesus Christ, letting their light shine in the world so that men are led to praise God. This, by the grace of God, they should be and do. Rather, I am pointing to that which only the eye of faith can see and the mind of faith discern, the presence of God with his chosen people.

Further, I am not saying that the organization and ethos of the local church do not matter. The better these are, the more readily the essence will be experienced within the congregation and its activities.

INVISIBLE AND VISIBLE

At this stage some readers, who are familiar with the contents of traditional Protestant textbooks on theology, may be assuming that the expression "invisible Church" is much the same as what I have called the essential nature of the Church, and "visible churches" is much the same as what I have called the historical existence of the Church as local congregations of sinful people in whom dwells the Holy Spirit. Such an assumption would be wrong. I must explain why.

The distinction between the Church as invisible and the Church as visible was originally made by Protestant theologians who wanted to show that the true Church of God was not equivalent to the massive Roman Catholic Church with its hierarchy and institutionalism. They argued that God in heaven who perfectly viewed both Roman and Protestant Churches knew exactly who in their membership were true believers (the elect) and thus members of the true Church of Christ. This true Church was therefore visible to the all-seeing God, but invisible to finite men. To enter this invisible Church, a person had to have spiritual birth from above. Protestant theologians also held that visible churches—that is, local congregations in parishes—were composed of both genuine, true believers and nominal, false believers. There was probably no pure local church whose total membership also had membership in the invisible Church. And in the case of Roman Catholic congregations, it was held that few if any members were truly born again and thus members of the invisible Church.

This distinction possibly has some usefulness today, but in the main it is misused, especially by evangelical Christians. For example, some use it as a justification for the activity of certain organizations and societies which function wholly independently of the local churches. The idea is that the invisible Church is primary and people enter it by being born again, and so integration into the programs of local churches is not necessary or even advisable. In the New Testament, as I hope will become clear by the argument of this book, what is primary for Christians is the local church, the church in Corinth or Rome or Jerusalem. This local church is "God's building." Where independent Christian societies exist, their duty is to work with the local churches and for the improvement and expansion of these churches.

So I would maintain that the invisible Church, the total company of all true believers of all times and places, is not the same as the Church viewed from the point of view of its essence. The essence or nature of the Church, while certainly being the God-dimension, necessarily exists within and through the human-dimension. The Christian who believes, or believes in, the Church sees the essence with the eye of faith in the actual historical existence and activity of the believing community. On the other hand, the total number of visible churches appears to be much the same as the historical existence of the one Church in many congregations. However, the main point remains that the distinction between invisible and visible and between essence and historical reality is not the same.

CONCLUSION

In several ways I have attempted to emphasize that the human community we call the church is in fact "God's church." In the local congregation the God-dimension and human-dimension are so integrated and intertwined that they cannot be separated. If a church is dissolved, then both essence and form are gone. If a church becomes heretical, denying the deity of Christ, the form remains, but the essence changes. The letters to the seven churches in Revelation 2, 3 reveal that churches can be in different states of commitment and loyalty, but even the erring church remains the church of God.

To be clear about the nature or essence of the Church is the way to begin to develop clear ideas as to its function in the world. This we shall attempt in the following chapters. Here I offer a few thoughts for the reader to consider. If I merely regard the church as a useful organization helping to keep society aware of goodness and morality, then I show myself unaware of the true reality of the church as belonging to God. If I regard membership in a local congregation as an optional extra to my Christian faith, then I show myself ignorant of what is God's saving purpose in history. If I think that I can disregard the existence of local churches and found a new church or house-fellowship (whatever supposed good reason I may have), then I show myself unwilling to accept that the church is not mine or ours, but God's. And if I believe that the way a church is organized, worships, and serves is neutral or of no consequence, then I fail to appreciate that the better the form of the local church, the more readily will the essence of the Church be known through and in the form. When, as a new convert or new resident, I have to choose to belong to a local church, I have to give careful consideration to its form—organization, worship, service, etc.—for certain traditions and expressions are more wholesome than others. My own view is that the Episcopal tradition, functioning properly and rightly understood, is the form which expresses best the essence of the Church.

QUESTIONS FOR DISCUSSION

1. Since the Corinthian congregation had so many faults, on what grounds could Paul *truthfully* call it God's church? What does your answer reveal in terms of the relationship of essence and form in the church?

2. In what circumstances is it helpful to distinguish the visible and invisible church?

3 LOOKING BACK

Christianity and Judaism are based on the belief that God has acted within human history and that this action can be identified in terms of people, places, and dates.

In the Old Testament a fundamental part of the liturgy of the Temple, of the teaching of the prophets, and of the piety of the Israelites was the regular recalling of the Lord's righteous activity in history. This is especially evident in the Psalms. For example:

Many times he delivered them,
  but they were bent on rebellion
  and they wasted away in their sin.
But he took note of their distress
  when he heard their cry;
for their sake he remembered his covenant
  and out of his great love he relented.
He caused them to be pitied
  by all who held them captive.
                    (106:43-46)

In practice this meant their deliverance! And this was through historical events.

At the annual celebration of the Passover, the head of

the house told his family the story of the deliverance from Egypt as they ate the lamb and bitter herbs (Exodus 12:25-27). In looking back to the mighty act of God in the Exodus, the participants believed that the same Savior was their God and he was able to do for them what he had done for their fathers. They looked ·back in order to look up.

As Isaiah had called the people to look back to Abraham and Sarah (Isaiah 51:2), so Paul urged the Christians of Galatia and of Rome to look to Abraham as the man of true faith in God (Galatians 3; Romans 4). The writer to the Hebrews recalled a long list of persons of faith in the Old Testament (Hebrews 11). When the apostles preached the Good News, they claimed that in specific persons and in specific events God had acted to save his people, bringing forgiveness of sins and everlasting life. The gospel is the declaration and proclamation that God was present in Jesus of Nazareth and that God acted in him, especially in his atoning death and glorious resurrection and ascension. Paul was quite clear on the factual, historical basis of the gospel—". . .that Christ died for our sins according to the Scriptures, that he was buried, that he was raised on the third day according to the Scriptures, and that he appeared to Peter, and then to the Twelve" (1 Corinthians 15:3-5).

One major aspect of the Eucharist or Lord's Supper is historical remembrance, which is done as part of the means by which God feeds our hearts with spiritual food. When he instituted the holy Supper, Jesus took bread, gave thanks, broke, and distributed saying, "This is my body, which is for you; do this in remembrance of me." Likewise he took the wine saying, "This cup is the new covenant in my blood; do this, whenever you drink it, in remembrance of me" (1 Corinthians 11:23-26). We cannot look up to the exalted Lord in heaven unless we also look back to see what he has done for us. His death upon the cross was an historical event which has everlasting significance.

Looking back, calling to remembrance, and recollecting not only presuppose that God's action is identifiable in past historical events; they also presuppose a continuity of persons associated with these events. Since the institution of the Lord's Supper, millions of people in many different places have week by week been calling to remembrance the death of the Savior. There is *one* community which began with the call of Abraham (Genesis 12). It was originally Hebrew, is still growing in numbers, and will continue to grow until the return of the Lord Jesus. At the center of this community is Jesus of Nazareth, the Incarnate Son of God. Those from Abraham to John the Baptist looked forward to him (Hebrews 11), and those from the apostolic age to the present look back to him. The history of this community is told in the Old Testament and the Apocrypha (from Abraham to the time of Jesus), and in the New Testament and books on Church history (from Jesus to the present).

There is of course a difference in status between the New Testament and books on Church history; the one is divinely inspired and authoritative for faith and life while the others, however excellent in method, content, and style, remain human in quality.

However, the main point here is that Israelite and Christian faith presuppose one continuous community in and through history, which at first was equivalent to a nation and since the apostolic period has been made up of people of many nations. "There is neither Jew nor Greek, slave nor free, male nor female, for you are all one in Christ Jesus," claimed Paul (Galatians 3:28). Becoming a Christian today means taking membership in a community with a long history. We look to its history covered by the Bible as the arena in which God revealed himself for all time, and we look to the history of the Church since the apostolic age as the arena in which God has helped his community to understand his revelation and to live by it.

Living in the final quarter of the twentieth century, we cannot ignore the fact that there has been a Christian Church in the world, and particularly in the Mediterranean and Western nations, for nineteen centuries and a half. As our family trees exist and usually can be traced, so God's family exists as a continuous community and has been traced. Before we consider some of the consequences of its continuous existence through the centuries for the present form of the Church, let us examine more images of the Church, images of continuity and of stability.

IMAGES OF CONTINUITY

The following images have as their primary thrust the idea of the continuity of those who truly believe in the Lord.

People of God

We use the word "people" in a general and perhaps vague way. We refer to a large crowd and say, "There were 10,000 people at the Billy Graham Crusade." We refer to the looting of shops in a city after an earthquake, hurricane, or war and say, "People act like that."

In New Testament times the use of the Greek word *laos* ("people") was normally for a specific group—a race, clan, tribe, or caste—bound together by ties of blood and social, economic, and cultural relations. For a person to move from one *laos* to another was rare, for it involved a radical change of status and life-style. For a person to be disowned by his people was a terrible fate, for he now belonged to nobody. Thus "a people" had a real existence and within the great Roman Empire there were many peoples, each of whom could be distinguished from the others, as the Romans well knew.

Thus, for there to be a people of God there had to be the divine initiative in creating this people, as well as the distinguishing marks to set this people apart from other peoples. This is what we find in the use of the image by Peter and Paul. Peter wrote that "you are a chosen people . . . a people belonging to God. . . . Once you were not a people, but now you are the people of God; once you had not received mercy, but now you have received mercy" (1 Peter 2:9, 10). He proceeded to show that one of the distinguishing marks of the people of God was their life-style, which was pure and holy.

Paul quoted from Hosea 2:23 and 1:10 and wrote, " 'I will call them "my people" who are not my people; and I will call her "my loved one" who is not my loved one,' and, 'It will happen that in the very place where it was said to them, "You are not my people," they will be called "sons of the living God" ' " (Romans 9:25, 26). In the context, Paul is referring to Gentiles being called the people of God along with believing Jews. But once more it is the divine mercy and initiative in creating the "people" which is emphasized. By this divine act individuals are called into a specific people, an identifiable people, the "people of God."

Of course it is true that in the final analysis only God can define the limits of his people, and he alone knows exactly who they are. (This is the truth in the idea of the Church as invisible, discussed in Chapter Two.) We know, however, from God's own revelation that from our human standpoint we are to see his "people" as the children of Israel before Christ and as the Church after Christ. This thought is clearly conveyed by the next image.

Israel

This was the name which God himself gave to Jacob after the famous wrestling match (Genesis 32:28). In later history "Israel" became the equivalent of "children of Jacob (Israel)," meaning the descendants of Jacob (Israel)—e.g., Deuteronomy 6:3, 4; 9:1; 20:3.

The most dramatic use of the word in the New Testament occurs in the letter to the Galatian churches. Their members were being troubled by Judaizers who wanted to impose Jewish ritual requirements on Gentile Christian believers. Paul vehemently opposed this and proceeded to tell the baptized but uncircumcised members that they were the "Israel" of God. Concluding his letter he affirmed, "Neither circumcision nor uncircumcision means anything; what counts is a new creation. Peace and mercy to all who follow this rule, even to the Israel of God" (Galatians 6:15, 16). Elsewhere Paul spoke of "citizenship in Israel" (Ephesians 2:12), and the writer to the Hebrews, quoting from Jeremiah 31:31ff., called the people of God the "house of Israel" (8:8-10). Without doubt this image highlights the continuity of God's people in the old and new covenants, which are seen as two administrations of one covenant of grace. This continuity is maintained despite the divine rejection of the nation of the Jews for its own rejection of the Messiah. As God created this "people of Israel," he also sets its limits and it pleased him to make his "people" predominantly of Gentile birth from the apostolic age onwards. (This rejection of the nation of Israel is the problem with which Paul wrestles in Romans 9—11. Whether he there actually teaches that before the end of the age large numbers of Jews will accept Jesus as the Messiah is a matter of debate among theologians, and has been so for a long time.)

"Chosen people" and "holy nation"

These two images are used by Peter in a passage (1 Peter 2:9) to which reference was made in the last chapter. "Chosen" points to the initiative of God in calling and choosing his own people. Likewise, "nation" has a meaning similar to "people" or "race," while the adjective "holy" points to the fact that it belongs to the holy Lord and is set apart for his own purposes. Both images portray the continuity of God's people in the Old and New Testament.

"Abraham's seed" and "Abraham's offspring"

These images are used by Paul as he recalled the basic promise the Lord made to Abram. He was commanded to leave his father's household and go to the land which the Lord was preparing for him, and to him God said:

"I will make you into a great nation
   and I will bless you;
I will make your name great,
   and you will be a blessing.
I will bless those who bless you,
   and whoever curses you I will curse;
and all peoples on earth
   will be blessed through you."

(Genesis 12:2, 3)

According to this, Abraham would have two types of descendants: first, those who were his blood descendants, the tribes of Israel; secondly, those from the peoples of the earth, who were blessed through him. The latter is interpreted by Paul in both Galatians and Romans as meaning those who had a faith like his, a faith which took God at his word and believed and obeyed him on the basis of it. Jesus, a blood descendant of Abraham, was the One who gave this promise its universal application. To the Roman church Paul writes, "Therefore, the promise comes by faith, so that it may be by grace and may be guaranteed to all Abraham's offspring—not only to those who are of the law but also to those who are of the faith of Abraham. He is the father of us all" (4:16). As Abraham, the man of faith and faithfulness, is the father of us all—Israelites and Christians—we are his "offspring" and "seed." To the Galatian churches Paul wrote, "If you belong to Christ, then you are Abraham's seed, and heirs according to the promise" (3:29). This image clearly highlights the truth that there is one people of God, a people which began with Abraham, centers on Christ, and is still in the world today as the Church.

IMAGES OF STABILITY

There are two of these, and they occur in one sentence written by Paul to his assistant, Timothy: "I write this . . . to let you know how men ought to conduct themselves in God's household, that is, the church of the living God, the pillar and bulwark of the truth" (1 Timothy 3:15, *NEB*). Having used the image of "household," his thought turned to buildings and he described the church as a "pillar" and "bulwark" of the truth (there are no definite articles in the Greek text).

How, it may be asked, can the Church, which is itself built upon Christ who is the Truth, also be a pillar and bulwark of the truth? The answer is that in the pastoral letters (1 and 2 Timothy, Titus) the word "truth" is used to mean the content of the Christian faith expressed in carefully chosen words, the orthodox faith as we say today—see 1 Timothy 4:3, 6:5; 2 Timothy 2:15, 18, 3:8, 4:4; Titus 1:14. It is the truth as the opposite of erroneous and heretical teaching. Paul described the false teachers and heretics as those who had lost grip of the truth (1 Timothy 6:5) and turned their backs upon the truth (Titus 1:14). So the local church is a pillar and bulwark of the truth when it defends orthodoxy against heresy and error. Much the same was claimed by Jude when he spoke of the struggle for the faith and of defending the faith (Jude 3).

What Paul is teaching is that as the pillar holds up the walls and the roof of the building, so each local church is to hold up the truth of the Christian faith so that each member, as well as outsiders, may know what actually is the orthodox faith and where it differs from heresies and errors. Also, as a bulwark or buttress (these are better translations of the Greek, *hedraioma,* than "foundation" or "ground" as in *AV* and *NIV*), each local church is to be a substantial defense of the orthodox faith against all attacks upon it. Thus each church is to teach with clarity and defend with zeal the orthodox faith of the Lord Jesus especially, as the pastoral letters show, teaching about the Lord Jesus himself and the salvation he brings.

It is surely a reasonable development of Paul's teaching here to claim that in each generation and each period of history local churches in all places are to preserve and hand on the Scriptures (from where the truth is learned), and also to preserve and hand on the orthodox faith (which is the best interpretation of the Scriptures at which the churches can arrive). Of course, churches have failed to live up to this calling and will fail again, but nevertheless it remains as part of their calling. Some continuity is implied in this general idea, for the Scriptures have to be passed on safely from generation to generation and the understanding of them at which the churches have arrived also has to be handed on. Of course, the understanding will in some cases improve and in other cases will be adapted to new situations and expressed in new languages.

HISTORICAL CONTINUITY

We have seen that there is continuity between the people of the old and new covenants, and that this community has the one Lord. Also, we have seen that the relationship of each church to the truth of God requires an identifiable continuity of churches through history.

The question we now face is, What kind of continuity should we expect to be believed, confessed, and practiced by the Church today? If we think again of the distinction between the essence and form of the church the question becomes, What relationship to the Church of earlier generations should there be in the Church today so that the local church may express as fully as possible the biblical idea of God's people as one people in history?

Many Protestants and Evangelicals have answered this question by claiming that we can ignore the history of the Church from the end of the apostolic age until the Reformation of the sixteenth century or even to modern times. All we need to do, they say, is to model churches today on biblical principles. God teaches us everything from Scripture and nothing or very little from the study of the mind of the Church over the centuries.

What I want to argue is that we must take seriously the existence of the Church from the first to the twentieth century. Our brothers and sisters in Christ have worshiped the Lord with deep devotion over the centuries, and we cannot ignore them or their worship. They belong to us as modern believers belong to us, for we all belong to the Lord Jesus. We take seriously the history of the people of God from Abraham to John the Baptist not only because we believe that God chose to reveal himself to them, but also because we belong to the same people of God as they do. We are all Abraham's children. Certainly the Old Testament books present us with an imperfect people, a backsliding people, an erring, sinful, and disobedient people, but nevertheless God's people.

In a similar way, the history of the Church is the history of an imperfect people with both good and bad pastors and confessing both wholesome and erroneous doctrines; yet the Church is God's people. When we recite the Nicene Creed, we affirm the historical reality of the Church. We affirm that the Church through history is *one* (for God's people is one), *holy* (for the Holy Spirit indwells), *catholic* (for God's people have been and are of many peoples), and *apostolic* (for God's people of the new covenant are founded upon the apostles and their teaching).

As we survey the history of the Church over the centuries, I believe that we can claim that in the providence of God certain features have been the means of reflecting or exhibiting its historical continuity. We must now look at the important features.

The Church as custodian of the Scriptures

From the Jews the first Christians received the collection (canon) of books we call the Old Testament, and for many years this was the only Bible in the Church. It was the Bible of the apostles and of Jesus. In the second century, the churches collected those documents which they believed had an apostolic origin and eventually the collection (canon) we call the New Testament emerged and gained acceptance. Before the collection was available, churches used parts of it and also relied upon the details of the gospel passed on by the apostles to their successors (i.e., oral tradition). So what we call the Bible was only in regular use from the third century onwards. This was preserved by the churches and copies of it made by scribes for circulation. Some translations were also made, into Latin for example. When the Roman Empire collapsed and throughout the so-called dark age of European history, the Church preserved copies of the Scriptures. The originals by Peter, Paul, Luke, and John were lost, but reliable copies were preserved and read.

So at one and the same time the Church preserved the Scriptures and read them as the final authority for faith and morals. The Church was under the authority of the Scriptures as well as acting as a bulwark to protect them from harm.

In modern times the Church has continued to act as the guardian of the Scriptures in that various translations have been undertaken and authorized. Behind these there lies much scholarly, patient endeavor. The King James Version of 1611, as well as its revision of 1885 known as the Revised Version, were authorized by the Church of England. The *Revised Standard Version* of 1952 was produced by a committee from the major Protestant churches of North America, while the *New English Bible* (1970) was produced by a team from the major Protestant churches of Great Britain. The *New International Version* (1978), which is being quoted in this book, was sponsored by the New York International Bible Society and so lacks the wide sponsorship of the others. However, the Society sponsored it in order that it be used in the Church, where its accuracy and usefulness will eventually be determined. I have used it because, being new, a lot of people are reading it at this time.

Paraphrases or translations made by individuals—e.g., J. B. Phillips or Ken Taylor—have been helpful to thousands of people in God's providence; but they reflect the ideas only of their creators, and so are not always reliable or accurate renderings of the original.

To claim that the Church is the custodian of Scripture is not to claim that at all times and in all places the Church has performed this duty with wisdom or zeal. Certainly the Church has failed in the past and continues to fail. For example, John Wycliffe (d. 1384) was right to condemn the Church for not making the Bible or parts of it available in the common language of the people.

The Church as guardian and teacher of orthodox doctrine

Within thirty years of the ascension of Jesus, Paul was conscious of the need for Timothy to defend Christian doctrines—i.e., the orthodox faith (see 1 and 2 Timothy). The Church regularly found this to be the case, and especially so in the great crisis caused by the teaching of Arius in the period from A.D. 320. Arianism denied that Jesus of Nazareth was the eternal Son of God in human flesh and claimed he was the incarnation of an angel. The bishops of the churches had to respond, and they produced in the ecumenical councils of Nicaea (325) and Constantinople (381) what we call the Nicene Creed. In it they confessed that Jesus Christ is "one in being with the Father" and "true God from true God." They also confessed the deity of the Holy Spirit, thereby affirming the doctrine of the Trinity, one God in three Persons.

Later the Church had to attempt to settle the problem of how Jesus could be one Person and yet be both human and divine. At the Council of Chalcedon (451), the bishops prepared a carefully devised formula, known as the Chalcedonian Definition, in which they affirmed that though he had two natures, human and divine, nevertheless he was one Person. This teaching found its way into the Athanasian Creed, which has been widely used in European churches.

So the Church of the fifth century passed on to the Church of the sixth century not only the Scriptures, but also its understanding of the Scriptures in terms of the doctrine of the deity of Jesus Christ, the Holy Trinity, and the unity of the human and divine natures in Jesus. Other doctrines were passed on as well—doctrines of the Church, ministry, and sacraments, for example. Not all doctrines passed on from generation to generation have stood the test of time and of reexamination. The doctrines of the Nicene Creed and Chalcedonian Definition certainly have done, but in other areas the Church modifies its understanding as it gains fresh light from Scripture.

It is the duty of the Church in all generations to read, interpret, and obey the Word of God. This should be done in the light of that understanding which is passed down in the Church in official doctrines, liturgies, devotional aids, biblical commentaries, and theological tomes. It is the duty of the Church at all times to test and check its understanding of God's salvation by fresh reading of Scripture. Being human and imperfect, the Church fails to live up to her high calling and so it is often the case that error or half-truth passes for sound doctrine. The Reformation of the sixteenth century became necessary because too much error and too many half-truths were in the medieval Church. Regrettably, the Reformation was the means by which the western catholic Church divided into Roman Catholic and Protestant, and Protestants divided amongst themselves.

Protestant Churches took much from the medieval Church. For example, the Apostles', Nicene, and Athanasian Creeds, the different forms of teaching on predestination and free will, and the need for sound learning in the universities controlled by the Church. Some Protestant Churches took over further features. The Church of England, for example, took over (with revisions) the medieval liturgy and also the threefold order of ministry of bishops, priests (presbyters), and deacons.

The succession of ordained ministers

Here I refer to what is commonly called "apostolic succession." This may be understood in a "high" and a "low" sense. The "high" version, for which the term "apostolic succession" is itself usually reserved, is that Christ ordained the apostles, the apostles ordained their successors (bishops) who in turn ordained or consecrated their successors, and so the succession has continued through the centuries. Thus, a Roman Catholic bishop anywhere in the world may claim to be in the apostolic succession, being able to trace his "pedigree" back through the centuries. With this version goes the idea of divine grace for effectual ministry being passed on with or by the laying on of hands. Historically this version is difficult to prove, for we have so little information about the century immediately following the apostolic period. Certainly by about A.D. 200 there was a threefold ordained ministry in the churches of bishops, priests, and deacons. Bishops ordained priests and deacons, while a bishop was consecrated by other bishops.

The "low" version, commonly called the "historic episcopate" view (which I personally hold), recognizes that very early in the history of the Church the threefold ministry became the norm, that this order of ministry continued through the years to the Reformation without change, and that from that time onwards it continued in some churches and not in others (e.g., in Roman Catholic, Anglican, and some Lutheran). It claims that God has led the Church into this form of ministry, and that having been well tried it should be retained in the Church. So, where there are schemes for reunion of churches (as there have been in South India, North India, etc.) then the episcopate should be restored. No special grace is conveyed by this historical succession, but the succession itself witnesses to the historical continuity and unity of the people of God.

Where the episcopal succession ceased, as for example in the Protestant State Churches of Germany and Scotland, there nevertheless remained a form of succession of ordained ministry. The first Protestant clergy had been ordained by bishops of the old Church, and they proceeded to ordain their successors in an orderly manner. This procedure has continued into the present. In a sense, it is also continued in those Churches which have grown from these State Churches—the Presbyterian and Lutheran Churches of North America, for example. The point I would make is that this form of succession does not witness as powerfully as does the succession of bishops to the historical nature of the Church. However, where you have a separatist or independent congregation, then the pastor can hardly be said to be in any kind of succession.

It may be asked, Does the acceptance of apostolic succession mean the recognition of the Pope? To accept the succession of bishops is to accept the bishopric of Rome, for the names of the bishops of Rome are known from the very earliest times. And as this bishopric has always been prominent in the life of the Church in western Europe, this must be recognized, just as the antiquity of the archbishopric of Canterbury, England has to be recognized. But that the Pope is the Vicar of Christ on earth and that he is the actual successor of the apostle Peter are doctrines which can only be accepted if Scripture clearly points to them, and in my view it does not do so.

The use of liturgy

If services (e.g., the Eucharist and services of Baptism and Evening Prayer) use structure and some content (e.g., Creeds) produced by former generations, then churches not only benefit from the wisdom of their forefathers, but also confess to the unity of the people of God through history in worship. Certainly services of worship need to be revised to meet changing cultural and linguistic patterns; yet the very act of revision, if done wisely, should testify to the historical continuity of worship by God's people, for that which has been used for generations is being adapted for use for further generations. I find that the use of liturgies which have historical depth helps me the more wholeheartedly to confess that "I believe in the communion of saints. . . ."

To say all this is not to deny any place in the life of the churches for extempore worship or for experimental liturgies. It is merely to affirm that we cannot abandon or neglect that which has been around for a long time merely to satisfy the whims of the present (which is often a short present). We shall return to the subject of liturgy in the next chapter.

The baptism of babies born to Christian parents

There is one covenant of grace which we think of as in two parts, the Mosaic or old covenant and the new covenant. In the old covenant as well as in the period from Abraham to Moses, circumcision was the sign of membership of the covenant (see Genesis 17). It was God's covenant sign, signifying God's movement in grace toward man, and it was from the human standpoint a sign of consecration to God. It was administered only to males because they were seen as the heads of families, and so they received the sign on behalf of their womenfolk as well.

In the new covenant the sign of membership is baptism. This, like circumcision, is primarily God's sign, his seal that the one being baptized belongs to him as his child. Again, from the human standpoint it is an act of dedication to God through Christ. Baptism is administered by the Church to believers and to the babies of believers. In missionary situations (of which the apostolic age is an excellent example), there are many converts and so there are many baptisms of believers. But where there is a settled church with Christian families, then there are baptisms of babies as well. The reality of the one covenant of grace and the fact of the one people of God require the Church to administer the sign of the covenant to the children of covenant members. While

only boys received the covenant sign in the old covenant, boys and girls receive it in the new covenant, for in
the new there is a greater display of the grace of God.

It is true that there is no obvious, indisputable evidence in the New Testament for the actual baptism of a
baby, but this is what I would expect in a missionary
situation. However, what there is not found in the New
Testament is a command from Jesus or one of his apostles forbidding the giving of the new covenant sign to
babies born to members of the new covenant. If the
Lord intended to abandon the practice existing from
Abraham to Christ—namely, giving the covenant sign to
the babies of believers—he would have made it clear. As
it was, the baptism of babies became common in the
churches after the apostolic period, and its continuance
through the centuries is a reminder to us of the continuity in history of the one people of God.

CONCLUSION

I must now summarize the answer I have given to the
question concerning how the local church may express
the fact of the historical unity of the one people of God.
I would expect a church to be related to other churches
of the past and present in a meaningful way—e.g.,
through a diocesan structure—and preferably through
the historical succession of bishops. Further, the church
should see itself (along with others) as the guardian not
only of the sacred Scriptures, but also of the interpretation of them passed on in the life of the Church. In so
viewing itself it would seek to be submitted to the authority of the same Scriptures. Also, it should worship
God in a way which both reflects the wisdom and experience of the centuries and is suitable for its own position. Finally, it should be a church which receives the

infants of believers through holy baptism as members of the one people of God.

QUESTIONS FOR DISCUSSION

1. Is it a good method to use the history of Israel, as recorded in the Old Testament, as a model for understanding historical continuity in the Church?

2. Does the variety of translations and paraphrases available today help or hinder believers in their attempt to form a doctrine of the Church?

4 LOOKING UP

To look up is to worship. The Church exists to look up to God in worship and to receive from him grace. Those images of the Church in the New Testament which we shall examine, while not always being easy to understand, point to this fundamental aspect of the life of the Church. In the primitive Church, worship was focused on the Lord's Day through the celebration of the Lord's Supper. Over the centuries this pattern has been developed, and the Eucharist remains today the central point of corporate worship as the Church looks up to God.

I realize that the metaphor of "looking up" could suggest the idea of a three-decker universe, but I use it as a metaphor. Therefore, it suggests looking away from creation to the Creator, away from the temporal to the eternal, and away from the finite to the infinite. It is a metaphor used in the Bible.

The people of God of the old covenant were urged to look to God, the LORD, their Creator and Redeemer. The Psalmist prayed in these words:

I lift up my eyes to you,
   to you whose throne is in heaven.

As the eyes of slaves look to
    the hand of their master,
as the eyes of a maid look to
    the hand of her mistress,
so our eyes look to the LORD our God
    till he shows us his mercy.

(Psalm 123:1, 2)

As the spokesman of the LORD, Isaiah said,

"To whom will you compare me?
    Or who is my equal?" says the Holy One.
Lift your eyes and look to the heavens.
    Who created all these?

(40:25, 26)

To look to God is to look to the One who has no equal and whose greatness allows no comparison.

When he was faced with 5,000 hungry men and their families, "looking up to heaven, Jesus gave thanks and broke the (five) loaves" (Mark 6:41). He looked to the Father in faith so that five loaves and two fishes could become sufficient for a great crowd. Stephen, the martyr, looked away from his persecutors and murderers to heaven. "Stephen, full of the Holy Spirit, looked up to heaven and saw the glory of God, and Jesus standing at the right hand of God" (Acts 7:55). In doing this, he set the example for all Christians, for we are urged to "fix our eyes on Jesus, the author and perfecter of our faith, who for the joy set before him endured the cross, scorning its shame, and sat down at the right hand of the throne of God" (Hebrews 12:2).

Looking to God in worship and receiving from him grace is the truth to which the following images of the church point.

CULTIC IMAGES

Because the first Christians saw themselves as the continuation of the people of God of the old covenant, they made use of images drawn from the cultic center of Judaism, the city and Temple of Jerusalem. Yet in using these images of the people of the new covenant, the biblical writers transformed their meaning so that they pointed to the new order of divine reality for and within the Church. We shall look at the images of Jerusalem, the Temple, priesthood, sacrifice, and aroma (incense).

Jerusalem

This is used by three writers. Paul rejoiced that "the Jerusalem that is above is free, and she is our mother" (Galatians 4:26). The earthly Jerusalem still existed when he wrote this, but it was no longer the city of God. Jesus taught that it would be destroyed by the Roman armies (Matthew 24:15ff.). Thus, the true sphere where God dwelt among his people now was the *ekklesia,* the Church of God. Existing on earth, but originating in the will of the Father, the *ekklesia* looks to its exalted Lord in heaven. This new Jerusalem or place (sphere) where God dwells is thus "above" in the sense that its essence or true nature is from heaven. Only within this community, sustained from heaven, do we learn of the grace of God and of God's will for our lives; only in this community do we feed on Christ in our hearts by faith as we partake of the Lord's Supper; and only in this community are we taught the meaning of the Lordship of Christ in our lives. So the Church is our mother, by whom we are fed, nurtured, disciplined, and protected. The Church is also free in that her members are a people whose sins are forgiven and who are walking in the Spirit (Galatians 5:16ff.). We are not slaves of sin, of

Satan, or of the law of Moses, for in Christ we are free; thus we freely worship God.

The writer to the Jewish Christians, emphasizing the great privileges of the people of the new covenant, wrote, "You have come to Mount Zion, to the heavenly Jerusalem, the city of the living God. You have come to thousands upon thousands of angels in joyful assembly" (Hebrews 12:22). Here again the heavenly origin and the God-dimension of the Church are highlighted. As Jerusalem was meant to be the place in which God was worshiped according to his will by his chosen people, so the Church is the sphere and people from whom pure spiritual worship should arise to God. The Church is to join with angels and archangels and all the company of heaven to laud and magnify the name of the Lord.

John's vision in Revelation 21 places the new Jerusalem in the future, to be revealed at the end of the age, as part of God's final victory over Satan, sin, and death. "I saw the Holy City, the new Jerusalem, coming down out of heaven from God, prepared as a bride beautifully dressed for her husband" (verse 2). Paul had in mind the perfection of the Church at the end of the age when he spoke of "a radiant church, without stain or wrinkle or any other blemish, but holy and blameless" (Ephesians 5:27). John's use of this image emphasizes both the divine origin of the Church and its perfection after the judgment at the end of the age. Such a picture encourages what I shall describe later as the "forward look."

In summary, we may claim that this image of the holy city highlights four related truths—the continuity of God's people in the old and new covenants, the great blessings and privileges of the new covenant (Jeremiah 31:31ff.; Ezekiel 36:25ff.), the spiritual worship which the church is to offer, and the glorious perfection which is God's plan for the future. Our interest is here particularly in the idea of offering spiritual worship.

Temple

This image is used by Peter and Paul, but we shall postpone study of Peter's use of it until we look at the image of priesthood. Paul told the Corinthian congregation that they were "God's temple." He developed this idea in the letter to the church in Ephesus by presenting a picture of the building of the temple, made up of Christ as the cornerstone, the apostles and prophets as foundation stones, and all believers as living stones. Here the idea of the Church growing until it reaches its fullness at the end of the age is presupposed. However, even in the process of growth it is indwelt by God; "in Christ you too are being built together to become a dwelling in which God lives by his Spirit" (Ephesians 2:22).

At one and the same time the earthly Temple in Jerusalem was the place where God dwelt (and where he set his name) and the place where the covenant people offered their worship to God. The worship of the Temple was ceaseless, with sacrifices morning and evening. So this image highlights the dual character of the Church—the people in whom God dwells and the people whose primary task is to offer worship to God the Father through the Son.

Priesthood

Peter brought together the two images of temple and priesthood. "You also, like living stones, are being built into a spiritual house to be a holy priesthood, offering spiritual sacrifices acceptable to God through Jesus Christ" (1 Peter 2:5). Christians are both living stones and holy priests. Having used these two images Peter went on to combine two further images, those of chosen people (or holy nation) and royal priesthood. Within ancient Israel the priests were a part of the people, but in the new Israel all God's people are priests. "You are a chosen people, a royal priesthood, a holy nation, a people belonging to God, that you may declare the praises of him who called you out of darkness into his marvelous light" (1 Peter 2:9).

This image of priesthood is also used by John in Revelation 1:6 and 5:10. Both Peter and John were able to call the Church a royal priesthood—that is, priests serving the LORD KING—because they looked upon Christ as the great and unique High Priest. This way of thinking about Christ as the Mediator between God and man is developed and explained in the Letter to the Hebrews (e.g., 9:11ff. and 10:11ff.). Christ exercises his new and everlasting priesthood in heaven, and united to him the Church shares in his priesthood. This image highlights the following truths: believers have direct access to the Father through Christ; they are to offer spiritual sacrifices to the Father; they are to proclaim the Word of God (even as the Israelite priesthood proclaimed the law of Moses); and they are to represent the world before God in prayer and service (even as the Israelite priesthood prayed for the nation).

Sacrifice

Though Paul did not use the image of priesthood of the Church, he did use that of sacrifice. To the Roman church he wrote: "I urge you, brothers, in view of God's mercy, to offer your bodies as living sacrifices, holy and pleasing to God—which is your spiritual worship" (Romans 12:1). He saw Christian service in terms of sacrifice, whether it be his own ministry or the sacrificial giving of his converts. Of himself he wrote, "I am already being poured out like a drink offering, and the time has come for my departure" (2 Timothy 4:6; cf. Philippians 2:17 for a similar statement). Drink offerings were libations, wine poured out before God (see Numbers 6:17; 15:1-12). He also described the gifts sent to him by the Philippian church as "a fragrant offering, an acceptable sacrifice, pleasing to God" (4:18).

In Romans 15:15, 16 he connected his own "priestly duty" and offering with the conversion of the Gentiles. He saw himself as "a minister of Christ Jesus to the Gentiles with the priestly duty of proclaiming the gospel of God, so that the Gentiles might become an offering acceptable to God, sanctified by the Holy Spirit." Paul, as it were, acts as a priest in presenting to God a sacrifice which is made up of Gentile Christians who have been converted through his preaching. This living sacrifice (cf. Romans 12:1) is acceptable to God not because of what it is in itself (it is sinful humanity), but because the Holy Spirit sets it apart and sanctifies it. In other words, the Gentiles receive the Holy Spirit as they repent of sin, believe on Christ, and are baptized.

So we see that this image functions in much the same way as priesthood. The people of God, the Church, are an offering and sacrifice made to God in the Holy Spirit. They are this particularly as they worship God in spirit and in truth and as they serve him according to his will in the world.

Aroma

Paul shared with the Corinthian congregation the thought that "we are to God the aroma of Christ among those who are being saved and those who are perishing. To the one we are the smell of death; to the other, the fragrance of life" (2 Corinthians 2:15, 16). There was in the Temple an altar of incense, and each morning incense was burned on it (Exodus 30:1-10; Luke 1:8-10). Its sweet aroma symbolized the prayers and worship of the people rising to God. Paul claimed that the preaching of the gospel by himself and the Corinthian church released a fragrance, the fragrance of the knowledge of Christ (v. 14). This led him on to make the further claim that those who preached the gospel, being filled as they were with the fragrance of knowledge of Christ, were themselves as the pleasing aroma of incense to God. What is a beautiful aroma to those who are in Christ is a horrible smell to those who reject Christ.

This is not a simple image, but what it highlights is that a continuous function of the Church is to be filled with the knowledge of Christ and so to worship and serve God continually. Only as the Church relates to God and looks to him can it do his will on earth.

These five images clearly present us with a picture of the Church which *looks up* to the God of all grace. This looking up is, however, not confined to times of corporate worship, important as these certainly are. It is a constant gaze which covers the activity of the congregation and each member from Sunday to Saturday. All that Christians do is to produce a sweet fragrance which rises to heaven and pleases the Lord.

Remembering that the total life of the Church is to be offered to God, I want to focus attention on its corporate worship. I do this because here the tone is set and the ethos is created in which all other activities—e.g., evangelism, sick visitation, home Bible studies, youth clubs, etc.—are conducted. Therefore, on the basis of the truth of Scripture and learning from the wisdom of the Church over the centuries, I want to state what

should be the main principles governing congregational
worship on the Lord's Day.

THE PRIMITIVE CHURCH

The first Christians of Jerusalem attended the daily services of the Temple. They also had joyful meals together. "Every day they continued to meet together in
the temple courts. They broke bread in their homes and
ate together with glad and sincere hearts, praising God
and enjoying the favor of all the people" (Acts 2:46).
Probably they saw these meals as continuations of the
meals which the resurrected Jesus had eaten with his
disciples (e.g., John 21:13; Luke 24:40-43). He was not
physically present, but was there by the Holy Spirit:
"Where two or three come together in my name, there I
am with them" (Matthew 18:20).

This practice of visiting the Temple had to stop because Christianity became unacceptable to the Jewish
leaders. Saul of Tarsus began to persecute the churches,
Stephen died as a martyr (Acts 6:8ff.), and Christians
were scattered.

Outside Jerusalem, in the cities of the Roman Empire,
the new groups of Christians attempted to meet in the
synagogue, but this did not work out. Paul always attempted first to preach in the local Jewish synagogue,
but he was usually rejected by the local Jewish leaders.
So the converts to Christ from both Jews and Gentiles
began to meet away from the synagogue.

What happened in Jerusalem and elsewhere made it
necessary for the churches to develop their own distinctive worship for use in their homes or hired halls. Three
factors appear to have influenced this development dur-
ing the apostolic age. First of all, the basic ingredients of
the synagogue service were retained—readings from

the Scriptures (Old Testament), singing of psalms, praise of God, prayers, and a sermon (explaining the readings). To keep these made good sense, and there was no sound reason for discarding them. Secondly, the communal meal which celebrated the presence of the risen Lord was continued; it was often called the *agape* or love-feast. Thirdly, the specific commemoration of the sacrificial **and** atoning death of Jesus was made through the Lord's Supper, the symbolic meal which Jesus had instituted the day before his crucifixion. In some churches this symbolic meal was placed at the end of the communal meal (e.g., see 1 Corinthians 11:17ff.).

Christian worship was on Sunday, the day of the resurrection and so the Lord's Day (Acts 20:7-12). The Sabbath or Saturday was left to the Jews for their worship. Since the early churches seem to have had regular visits from evangelists and prophets, and also to have possessed in their own membership various gifts of the Spirit (1 Corinthians 12:7ff.), we must assume that there was a certain fluidity in worship. This proved both a strength and a weakness; a strength in that there was a possible richness of blessing and weakness in that there was opportunity for abuse (as Paul found, 1 Corinthians 14:6ff.).

Further developments took place at the end of the apostolic age as the churches became predominantly Gentile in membership and as Christianity was treated as illegal by the local Roman governors. One such servant of imperial Rome, Pliny of Bithynia, described Christian worship in one of his letters to the Emperor Trajan (Pliny *Epistles*, X, 96). It was written in A.D. 112. Pliny did not fully understand what he was describing. However, he wrote of a service held before dawn which included readings from Scripture (including the Decalogue, Exodus 20), singing of psalms, and probably the symbolic meal of the Lord's Supper (he used the word *sacramentum*). There was a further service at the end of the day when the daily work finished, and this took the form of an *agape*. Pliny stopped this as being illegal. The basic reason why the early service was held was to accommodate the members who were slaves, who had to work from dawn for their masters.

Here we note the beginnings of the fusion into one service of what were the basic ingredients of synagogue worship (i.e., the ministry of the Word) with the Lord's Supper. Also, the Lord's Supper is being separated from the *agape*. This development is confirmed by Justin Martyr, the Christian philosopher who worked in Rome. In his *First Apology* (Parts 65—67), written about A.D. 150, he described that which he knew as the regular worship of the Lord's Day. The service or liturgy began with readings from the Old Testament and one from the Gospels. This being ended, the local bishop, seated in his chair (cf. Luke 4:20), delivered his sermon. Prayers of the people followed. These included praise, thanksgiving, intercession, and petition, ending with a vigorous "Amen" said by all. Next came the symbolic expression of their fellowship in Christ, the exchange of the kiss of peace. The offertory followed, and this was the presentation of bread and wine by the congregation to the bishop. This was collected and arranged on the holy table by the deacons. The final part of the liturgy was the consecration prayer said by the bishop and the communion of the people who ate bread and drank wine in remembrance of the crucified Christ.

By this time the churches had what may be called a settled ministry, the threefold order of bishop, presbyters (priests), and deacons. City churches had their own bishop with several presbyters and deacons, but country congregations were served by one or two presbyters and deacons. Traveling preachers were becoming less common, and little use appears to have been made in public worship of the gifts of the Spirit.

Therefore, we see how the basic structure of the liturgy of the Lord's Day, the Eucharist, came into being. It was made up of the ministry of the Word (readings and sermon), prayers, fellowship, and the ministry of the sacrament, or the celebration of the Lord's Supper. Many writers, beginning with Hippolytus of Rome in his famous *Apostolic Tradition* (he died A.D. 236), record that this was the basic structure, which had of course local variations.

THE MODERN SCENE

Over the centuries this structure was retained, and other liturgical services were created for use on each day of the week. We are all aware of some of the abuses which crept into the Eucharist (or Mass), especially in the medieval period. Too much emphasis was placed on the ministry of the sacrament to the neglect of the ministry of the Word. Though the Church had believed from earliest times that in the Eucharist the bread and wine became Christ's Body and Blood, in a mystery, more and more this came to be understood in a gross and carnal way. Among the uninstructed there was talk of "bleeding Hosts" and other miraculous events connected with the consecrated elements. Worse, some of the faithful apparently thought the Eucharist was a re-crucifixion of Christ—though the Church never taught or held this. Such abuses (which the Church was either unable or unwilling to check), in the context of many others in the administration and ministry of the Church, made the Reformation of the sixteenth century virtually inevitable.

It was necessary for the Church in Europe to be reminded again of the dynamic teaching of the apostles recorded in Scriptures and of the example and teaching of the early fathers (e.g., Athanasius and Augustine). It was right that the Church should look at itself in the light of the Scriptures in order to be judged by God. It was good that earnest souls should be told how they might find salvation and assurance in Jesus Christ. It was helpful that the liturgy of the Church, and certainly the Eucharist, be examined.

Regrettably, the reformers (Calvin, Luther, Bucer, Cranmer, etc.) did not see eye to eye on the renewal of the liturgy. So different forms of service evolved in the Protestant tradition of the sixteenth century. And, to these, many further variations and additions came from the seventeenth to the twentieth centuries as the Protestant denominations divided and subdivided. Certain Protestant Churches—e.g., Anglican and Lutheran— did retain the basic structure of the Eucharist known through the centuries and made provision for its regular celebration each Lord's Day. They also reformed other parts of the weekly services and provided daily services of morning and evening prayer. The Roman Church not only retained the ancient structure of the Eucharist but also, despite some revisions by the Council of Trent (1545-1563), retained some of the medieval abuses. In recent times, especially since the Vatican Council of 1962-65, there has been further reformation of the liturgy, as is seen in the use of the vernacular everywhere. Revisions are also being made in the liturgies of Anglican and Lutheran Churches, with new books of services appearing.

ESSENCE AND FORM

As Christians wishing to be obedient to the Lord Jesus in today's world, we have to choose one of the many forms in which worship in God's Church is encountered in our society. In all these forms, from the independent Bible church to the Roman Catholic parish, we may encounter the essence or nature of the Church. That is, we may meet with God in Christ as he grants us his grace. But the form does matter, and so it is important to get as near as possible to that form which the more readily allows the worshipers to be in living relationship to the essence—that is, to the living God. Since corporate worship is at the center of the existence of the local church, the type of worship offered to God on the Lord's Day must be the best possible.

The proposal I make is that we should look for a church which uses each Lord's Day a basic liturgy of the Eucharist in which the ministry of Word and sacrament are present in a balanced way. Such a church, if it is living in the ethos of the Eucharist, will certainly be a church which *looks up* to its heavenly Father and exalted Lord. Its form will be true to its essence.

My proposal is based on three considerations. The first is the argument from tradition which is outlined above; I find it hard to believe that God's providence allowed the Church to get the main structure of the Eucharist wrong for fourteen centuries or more. The second is a realistic assessment of what happens when the order and content of the worship is left wholly in the hands of one man, the pastor. This is the case in many independent congregations, and in practice it means that the content of the service of worship is determined by the ability, knowledge, and spirituality of one man. If he is a godly, sensitive, and learned man, then he will produce a good form of worship; but we cannot expect all pastors to be of the highest qualities of mind and spirit! The third is an argument based on aesthetic appreciation. In the Eucharist, the salvation of God is presented in word and in symbol, to the ear and the eye; if a dignified ritual is associated with the Eucharist, then the whole drama—actions and words—is addressing us as whole people. We need not take over the whole ritual and ceremonial of high medievalism to appreciate the force of external drama, and to be taught and enriched by God through it.

It may be argued that my proposal is based on theory and that most churches, where there is the kind of liturgy and celebration of the Eucharist which I commend (e.g., in Episcopal churches), are "dead" or "liberal" or "lukewarm." Regretfully I accept that many churches do not live and act in the true spirit of the fine liturgy they use; but I would add that here in the liturgy is the basis for the church to become in practice what it is in worship, a church which looks up to God and honors him all the week in its words and deeds. If you join a supposed lukewarm church in humility, then perhaps the Lord by his Spirit will help you to become gradually a means of bringing the congregation to a deeper realization of the implications of its worship.

QUESTIONS FOR DISCUSSION

1. What are the implications for a local church which desires to function as a royal priesthood?

2. "Since God has given us five senses, the fullness of corporate worship should involve all and speak to all." Is this a reasonable assumption and is it fulfilled in the Eucharist?

5 LOOKING FORWARD

As I look out my window toward the center of London, what I can see is limited due to the haze and the limitations of human eyes. If I look forward into the future of Western society, the best I can envisage is an increasing dependence on technology and an uncertain peace. But when I look forward into time in the faith of Christ, believing the promises of God, I can see a wonderful sight—an age in which there is perfect fellowship and cooperation between God and man in a new kind of cosmos. What I can see as a man of faith I can only describe (as did the biblical writers) in symbols and metaphors, for the quality of the age to come is not easily put into plain terms. Christian hope, or the Christian view of the future, is often most clearly expressed in poetic language.

The reader of the Old Testament cannot miss there the unmistakable looking forward to a future age when the Lord would reign and the people cheerfully serve him. This hope is expressed in a variety of ways. There is talk of a new covenant between God and man (Ezekiel 36:26ff.; Jeremiah 31:31ff.), of a new universe (Isaiah

2; Micah 4), a purified Israel (Isaiah 40, 41), a glorious age ruled by the Messiah (Isaiah 9:6ff.; 11:1ff.), and the elimination of sin and all opponents of God (Psalm 2; 20; 21; 72; 110; etc.). Common to all these ways of expressing a hope for the future is the belief that God will decisively intervene in the history of the world.

The first Christians, following the teaching of Jesus, believed that many of the promises of the Old Testament were perfectly fulfilled in the life, death, resurrection, and ascension of Jesus and in the descent of the Holy Spirit. However, they believed that the climax of history was not yet reached, for the Lord Jesus was to return to earth in order to judge the world and raise the dead. The victory over Satan, sin, and death had been won, but the final subjugation of these enemies of God would occur at the end of the present evil age. So Christians had much to look forward to.

Paul told Titus, his "son" in the faith, that "we wait for the blessed hope—the glorious appearing of our great God and Savior, Jesus Christ, who gave himself for us to redeem us from all wickedness and to purify for himself a people that are his very own, eager to do what is good" (Titus 2:13, 14). To the church of Philippi the apostle affirmed that "our citizenship is in heaven. And we eagerly await a Savior from there, the Lord Jesus Christ, who, by the power that enables him to bring everything under his control, will transform our lowly bodies so that they will be like his glorious body" (Philippians 3:20, 21).

Peter emphasized both the negative and positive aspects when he wrote:

You ought to live holy and godly lives as you look forward to the day of God and speed its coming. That day will bring about the destruction of the heavens by fire, and the elements will melt in the heat. But in keeping with his promise we are looking forward to a new heaven and a new earth, the home of righteousness.

(2 Peter 3:11-13)

Here is the cosmic picture of a new kind of universe.

Paul claimed that "what is seen is temporary, but what is unseen is eternal" (2 Corinthians 4:18), while the writer to the Hebrews spoke of faith as "being sure of what we hope for and certain of what we do not see" (Hebrews 11:1). The element of looking forward in faith is prominent in the Eucharist. In this act of worship we look up to the exalted Savior, look back to his death upon the cross, and look forward to his return in glory and the establishment of his kingdom. "For whenever you eat this bread and drink this cup, you proclaim the Lord's death until he comes" (1 Corinthians 11:26).

So the Church looks forward in faith and hope to God's further righteous and saving activity, knowing that it will have a place in this activity. To explore this further, we look at two groups of images which present the Church in this perspective.

IMAGES OF PILGRIMAGE

The idea of the Christian community as a pilgrim people is deeply embedded in Christian literature—e.g., John Bunyan's *Pilgrim's Progress*—because it is clearly presented by a variety of forms in the biblical material. Here are two forms.

Strangers (exiles) in the world

Peter used this picture to present the community of Christians as estranged from, and in some cases rejected by, the pagan society in which they lived. "I urge you, as aliens and strangers in the world," he wrote, "to abstain from sinful desires, which war against your soul. Live such good lives among the pagans that, though they accuse you of doing wrong, they may see your good deeds and glorify God on the day he visits us" (1 Peter 2:11, 12).

The Letter to the Hebrews provides a second interpretation of this image. Here the way of life of Christians in the world is seen as a testimony to the fact that they belong to a different society and country. People of faith admit by their life-style that they are "aliens and strangers on earth" and are "longing for a better country—a heavenly one" (11:13, 16).

So we conclude that the Church on earth today is composed of exiles from our godless and materialistic society who are at the same time exiles from the future kingdom of the Lord Jesus in which they hold citizenship.

The dispersion

There were many Jews living in the towns and cities of the Roman Empire. Their forefathers had left Palestine in times of trouble, but while they looked to Jerusalem as their spiritual home and tried to visit it at festival time, they were usually content to stay outside Palestine. The dispersion was a word in common usage, and so when James and Peter used it their Jewish-Christian as well as Gentile-Christian readers would know its normal meaning.

James addressed his letter "to the twelve tribes scattered among the nations" (James 1:1), while Peter combined the images of strangers and the dispersion to write "to God's elect, strangers in the world, scattered throughout Pontus, Galatia, etc." (1 Peter 1:1). It is hardly likely that they were expecting the Christian communities to look to Jerusalem as their spiritual home as did the Jewish communities. They were thinking of the heavenly kingdom and city of the Lord Jesus, that Jerusalem which is above. Christians belonged to Christ in heaven and there their primary loyalty was, whether persecution or favor was shown them by people on earth.

The Church today remains a dispersed people, scattered much more widely than were the Jewish communities in A.D. 70. But the Church still looks for the heavenly city "whose architect and builder is God" (Hebrews 11:10).

COSMIC IMAGES

God is presented in the Bible as our Creator and Redeemer. His work as Redeemer is often a work of creation. The first creation is polluted by sin and so out of it he is making a new order, a new creation. Thus, it is not surprising that the people who are redeemed by God are described in terms associated with God as Creator or with his created order.

New creation

Paul described the whole Christian community (Galatians 6:15) and each member (2 Corinthians 5:17) as a new creation. It is clear that he felt able to use this picture because he understood the Church to be in vital union with Jesus Christ. By his atoning death and glorious resurrection, he triumphed over all the evil forces in the old creation and brought into being a new order, which will be finally and fully established when he returns in glory. The Church belongs to this new order of reality, not to the old order which is destined for judgment and destruction. Certainly the new order is a larger reality than the total people of God; but as this people is at the very center of the kingdom of God, the Church is rightly called a new creation.

First fruits

James explained that God "chose to give us birth through the word of truth, that we might be a kind of firstfruits of all he created" (1:18). Here the idea is of being born into a new creation which is not the whole, but the first fruits of the whole. For every Jew, "firstfruits" carried an instantaneous meaning because of its place in the Law of Moses. The first of the fruit to ripen was offered to the Lord in a spirit of indebtedness to him and in anticipation of the full harvest to follow (Exodus 23:19; Leviticus 23:10, 17; Deuteronomy 26:1-11). Similarly, the Lord had the first claim upon the offspring of men and animals (Exodus 13:2; 34:19; Leviticus 27:26; etc.). What James appears to be saying is that the Church is the first part, the first visible part, of the future kingdom of God to be seen and experienced in the present age. To look at the Church is to have God's sign and pledge of greater things to come, the fullness of the future reign of the Lord.

This image was used by Paul, and his usage may be seen as complementing that of James. Paul spoke of Christ as the first fruits in the sense of his being the pledge of the future resurrection of our bodies (1 Corinthians 15:20-23). Also, the Holy Spirit living in the hearts of believers is the pledge of the greater enjoyment of the presence of God in the age to come (Romans 8:23). And finally Paul described the first converts in a specific region as the first fruits of the larger numbers of converts in that region (Romans 16:5 and 1 Corinthians 16:15 in the *RV*).

A new man

This is used by Paul. To the Colossian church he wrote:

Lie not one to another; seeing that ye have put off the old man with his doings and have put on the new man, which is being renewed unto knowledge after the image of him that created him: where there cannot be Greek or Jew, circumcision and uncircumcision, barbarian, Scythian, bondman, freeman: but Christ is all and in all.

(Colossians 3:9-11)

And to the Ephesian church he wrote:

Put away as concerning your former manner of life, the old man, which waxeth corrupt after the lusts of deceit; and that ye be renewed in the spirit of your mind and put on the new man, which after God hath been created in righteousness and holiness of truth.

(Ephesians 4:22, 23)

I have used the *RV* here because it translates *anthropos* as "man," whereas the *NIV* uses the word "self."

Hebrew thought, which is reflected not only in the Old but also in the New Testament, moved freely from the idea of the individual to the idea of the community to which the individual belonged. Already we have seen that both an individual Christian and the Church are a "new creation." Here the "new man" is primarily a corporate, collective idea, but also it can be used of the individual Christian. So for "new man" we could say "new humanity" or "new race."

Paul was contrasting two men or two humanities. The old man is inseparably connected with a sinful, selfish behavior, while the new man is inseparably connected to pleasing God by being righteous, holy, and loving. And there is more. The old man is a humanity in which divisions of race, sex, culture, citizenship, and class are important and cannot be forgotten or neglected. They are real, and politicians and administrators have to face them. The new man is a humanity in which these divisions cannot ever be primary or important, for in Christ they are canceled.

In the Roman Empire one of the greatest barriers between human beings was the religious and social barrier that separated Jews and Gentiles. Paul claimed that this high cultural and religious wall had been abolished by Christ and should not exist in the Church. To the Ephesians he wrote:

For Christ himself is our peace, who has made the two one and has destroyed the barrier, the dividing wall of hostility. . . . His purpose was to create in himself one new man out of the two, thus making peace.

(Ephesians 2:14, 15)

Part of the reconciling work of Christ on the cross was to destroy barriers between human beings. He who reconciles us to God reconciles us to one another.

The image of the "new man" is further developed by Paul in the discussion in which he contrasted the first Adam (Genesis 2—3) and the second Adam (Jesus Christ). Both men represented a humanity before God, but whereas the first Adam involved his humanity in sin and death, the second Adam brought to his righteousness and life. See Romans 5:12ff. and 1 Corinthians 15:21, 22.

IMPLICATIONS FOR TODAY

If the context of the five images discussed above is examined, one fact at least becomes clear. The implication of the truth which all these images highlight is that God's people in each locality are to exhibit a total way of life which reflects that the age to come is their true home and that the Lord of that age is their present Savior and King. There is to be an obvious contrast between the life-style of those for whom earth is their true home and those for whom earth is the place of pilgrimage and exile. What matters is that the Church should be a community whose quality of life is obviously spiritually and morally superior (through divine grace) to that of the population in which they live.

I recognize that it is easy for a theologian to make general assertions such as these, and so I must try to be more specific in terms of explaining what the general assertion implies. Here are five implications:

The worship of the local church should be an anticipation of the glorious worship which the "new man" will offer to God in the age to come. This is more than the right association of words; it is an attitude of heart and mind as well as an ethos. In most liturgies for the Eucharist the right words are there. For example, in the new Church of England rite we say:

. . . Therefore with angels and archangels, and with all the company of heaven, we proclaim your great and glorious Name, for ever praising you and saying:
"Holy, holy, holy Lord,
God of power and might,
Heaven and earth are full of your glory,
Hosanna in the highest."

These words become the means of a vital faith when they are said or sung by a people who know they are pilgrims! One way to look at the Eucharist is to see it as a small feast which anticipates the great feast of the kingdom of God. We feed on Christ now in our hearts by faith and with thanksgiving, and thereby anticipate that spiritual feeding which will be our constant delight in the age to come. We meet now at the table of the Lord, knowing that we shall attend the royal banquet in the life hereafter. The old liturgy (1662) of the Church of England has the following words of administration: "The Body (or Blood) of our Lord Jesus Christ . . . preserve thy body and soul unto everlasting life. . . ." Here the resurrection is anticipated, and with it the life of the age to come.

The membership and fellowship of the local church must reflect the truth which is highlighted by the image of the "new man." In days of mass production, when quantity often seems more important than quality, many churches have succumbed to the misguided belief that if the membership grows, then they are being necessarily successful for God. We need to recognize that if we do not make large demands on converts, then we are the more likely to be numerically successful. If our aim is to produce churches in which different types of people by the grace of God are living in an integrated, harmonious way and beginning to reflect the life style of the new humanity, then we may not expand so quickly in terms of numbers. Indeed, the reason why so many "conservative" churches grow in North America is that they provide little or no challenge to the value systems adopted by the society in which they live. They offer heaven in a kind of package deal in which few probing demands are made on the life style of the average middle-class citizen. We want quantity with quality, but we must not go only for quantity, for in so doing we are in danger of losing the character of the Church as a holy and a pilgrim people. If we have to choose, quality must come first.

The involvement of the church in ownership of property, stocks, and shares need to be carefully monitored and controlled. I recognize that even a pilgrim people needs somewhere to worship God and have fellowship in the love of Christ. Likewise, other buildings are needed for church agencies and societies. Also, legacies left to the church have to be managed. So what I call for is an attitude of mind, an approach to the ownership of property and investment, which is truly meaningful for a pilgrim people who are exiles here on earth. Whatever property or investments the churches have should be managed well—in an exemplary way, wherever possible—but they are means to an end, which is the service of God. The question we should often be asking ourselves is: "How should our attitude to property be affected by our membership in the people of God whose primary loyalty is to the age to come?" This is not an easy question to answer, and answers should not be immediately implemented. Careful thought and prayer is needed to ascertain the mind of Christ in this area, and what is right for one situation will not necessarily be right for another.

Having experienced the grace of God and living in fellowship with him, a church will always want to minister to the society in which it is placed. Pilgrims will surely want to explain their pilgrimage and the place to which they go. Exiles will often speak of their homeland. Renewed men will tell of how they are renewed and what it means. But not only will the church speak, it will minister. One of the qualities of the life of the age to come is love, the love of God; pilgrims, exiles, new creatures, and new men have this love in their hearts, and this love is ever seeking needy persons on whom it can be fulfilled. The church which is too early for heaven and too late for earth will nevertheless be known on earth for its compassion and care. (We return to this subject in the next chapter.)

Since all Christians belong to "one man" and the "new cre-

ation," and since they will be together in the life of the age to come, they will see the unity of God's people here on earth as a goal toward which to move and work. For a variety of reasons, social and historical, the people of God are divided into different denominations which sometimes are in competition with each other. This situation cannot be right, even though we can give many seemingly sound reasons for its continuance. Further, to complicate matters, so much of the current ecumenical movement seems to be governed by principles which are contrary to biblical insights and perspectives. However, even though the official commissions and committees of denominations and of the World Council of Churches seem to be making little progress—or worse, getting involved in too much politics—we are surely required by Christ at the local level to do all we can in his name and love to bring into practice that unity which already he has gained for us by his cross and which the Spirit wishes to bring to us.

*   *   *   *   *

Each of these five implications of being a pilgrim people and a new creation needs to be worked out in detail in each different local situation. This means leadership being given by pastors and teachers, followed by the involvement of all the membership in developing a Christian life style for today. To expect perfection in each of these areas is to expect the fullness of the kingdom of God in the here and now. What we can realistically expect and work for is the acknowledgment of these implications and goals (or others carefully learned from Scripture) and the desire to move toward their realization. Do we not pray "Your will be done on earth as it is in heaven"? Only when the Church seeks to move toward these goals and lives the Christian life style in today's world will the essence of the Church be fully reflected in its form.

QUESTIONS FOR DISCUSSION

1. Is there a proper balance between quantity and quality in the Church, or should one of these be primary?

2. What Christian life style is appropriate for you, your family, and your friends?

6 LOOKING AROUND

As a tourist, I have found myself looking around many interesting places from Madras to Vancouver and from Rome to Capetown. What I see I usually interpret according to the advice of my guide or my guidebook.

As a prospective house buyer I have found myself looking around different houses with the serious intention of negotiating a sale. What I see I interpret in terms of my needs, current market values, position in relation to public transportation, quality of neighborhood, and so on.

When the Church looks around at the world, the members should interpret what they see with the eyes and mind of Christ. From this perspective, self-sufficient society is seen as needing the love of God revealed in Jesus Christ. Technological and scientific man is seen as needing spiritual regeneration and a divine calling and purpose in life. Affluent man is seen as needing God's riches of grace, and alienated man is seen as needing reconciliation to God and to human beings. What the Church sees as it looks around is that on which not only the eyes are to be focused, but the energy also is to be concentrated. To look becomes to care; to care becomes to act in love.

We look to Jesus for the example of looking around. In conversation with his disciples he urged, "Open your eyes and look at the fields. They are ripe for harvest" (John 4:35). In the context, he was speaking about cooperation in the work of the kingdom between those who sow and those who reap. To the seventy disciples whom he sent out to proclaim God's rule he also said, "The harvest is plentiful, but the workers are few" (Luke 10:2). To see the need in God's world is to take action, for love cannot remain indifferent to need. A further example is provided by Jesus in the way in which he looked at Jerusalem, the center of the worship of the old covenant. "As he approached Jerusalem and saw the city, he wept over it" (Luke 19:41). He looked; he wept; he entered; he taught; he suffered; he died; and he rose from death. Love must act.

The relation of the community of believers to the local society can be expressed in either personal or impersonal images.

PERSONAL IMAGES

Witnesses. This picture originates in the law court where certain persons give testimony to what they know and believe and to what they have seen and heard. For Luke, who wrote the Acts of the Apostles, the apostles and disciples who had been commissioned by the risen Jesus to proclaim the kingdom of God were witnesses. "You will receive power when the Holy Spirit comes on you; and you will be my witnesses in Jerusalem, and in all Judea and Samaria, and to the ends of the earth" (Acts 1:8). In particular, they were to be witnesses of the resurrection of Jesus (Acts 1:22). Their message was primarily of Jesus and what God had done in him, and in giving their testimony to Jesus they were to be ready to die. The word "witness" and "martyr" are intimately associated, so that Acts 22:20 may be translated "your martyr Stephen" or "your witness Stephen."

In the fourth Gospel, John the Baptist is presented as an important witness, for he clearly pointed to Jesus as the Messiah, "the Lamb of God who takes away the sin of the world" (John 1:7ff.). Also, the idea of witness is prominent in the presentation of Jesus as the eternal Son of God made man. What he did in terms of his ministry and miracles were witnesses to his true identity (John 5:36; 10:25). The Father who sent the Son bore witness to the real nature of Jesus by his involvement in what Jesus did (John 5:37). Also, the Hebrew Scriptures witnessed to Jesus by describing in advance what would be his mission (John 5:39). Finally Jesus himself claimed to be a witness to the truth (John 18:37); that is, to the truth that the Lord God loves and acts to save his people.

Building upon this rich use of the idea of witness, the disciples are presented as witnesses in a context concerning the Holy Spirit as the One who will continue the work of Jesus in the world after his ascension into heaven. Jesus said:

"When the Counsellor comes, whom I will send to you from the Father, the Spirit of truth who goes out from the Father, he will testify about me; but you also must testify, for you have been with me from the beginning."

(John 15:26, 27)

The Holy Spirit is the witness to the exalted Lord Jesus, and Christians, in whom is the Spirit, join in this testimony by what they are, do, and say.

The theme of witnessing is also prominent in the First Letter of John. In the introduction come the words, "We proclaim to you what we have seen and heard," and the content of this witnessing is provided in the later explanation, "We have seen and testify that the Father has sent his Son to be the Savior of the world" (1 John 4:14). In the Johannine Revelation Jesus is presented as the "faithful witness" (Revelation 1:5), and those who serve the Lord Jesus Christ faithfully in times of persecution are said to "hold to the testimony of Jesus" (Revelation 12:17).

What can be said of witnesses? They should be totally committed to that which they present or else are not likely to be believed. They should be held to account for the truthfulness of their testimony; witnesses must not commit perjury, but responsibly testify to the truth. Finally, they should present their case in a way which is meaningful to their hearers, adapted to local language and culture. Christian believers as witnesses of Jesus Christ are to be totally committed to him, to proclaim him on the basis of the revelation provided in Scripture, and to speak in ways which are convincing to their hearers.

Ambassadors. The role of an ambassador has not changed much since the time of Paul. He or she acts and speaks both on behalf of and in the place of the government which is represented. In this function he has no mind of his own, for he represents faithfully the message he has been given. Paul used this image when writing to Corinth:

God was reconciling the world to himself in Christ, not counting men's sins against them. And he has committed to us the message of reconciliation. We are therefore Christ's ambassadors, as though God were making his appeal through us. We implore you on Christ's behalf: Be reconciled to God.

(2 Corinthians 5:19, 20)

To reconcile is to bring two parties together. In Christ, by his saving acts, God has provided reconciliation between a sinful world and himself. This, however, has to be believed, received, and appropriated by needy sinners. This is why Paul spoke of "making his appeal" and "we implore you." The Church, as an ambassador to the world, has a message which is to be proclaimed urgently, faithfully, and lovingly, and it is a message of reconciliation.

Slaves. This will never be a popular image of the Christian community today, for we are not proud of the history of slavery in Europe and America. However, we need to remember that Jesus accepted that the relationship of a slave to his master was a good picture of the relationship of the disciple of the kingdom of heaven to God himself. He often used the institution of slavery in his parables and stories (see Matthew 13; 18; 22; 24; 25; Mark 12; Luke 14; 15; 20). He taught that "No one can serve two masters. Either he will hate the one and love the other, or he will be devoted to the one and despise the other. You cannot serve both God and Money" (Matthew 6:24). Later he told his disciples that "whoever wants to become great among you must be your servant, and whoever wants to be first must be your slave—just as the Son of Man did not come to be served, but to serve, and to give his life a ransom for many" (Matthew 20:26, 27).

Paul also described Christians as slaves of Jesus Christ. For him true freedom was found in perfect service of Jesus (Romans 6:18; Galatians 5:13ff.). The sinner is set free, Paul believed, for "the obedience of faith," which he presents to the Lord Jesus Christ as his servant and slave (Romans 12:11, 14:18; Colossians 3:24). Jesus himself took the form of a servant (Philippians 2:7), thereby setting the example of service by his Church, service to one another, and service to the world. Jesus had a ministry to his disciples, to the people of the old covenant, and to the world. As his slave, the Church continues this ministry to the world.

It hardly needs stating that a slave was a slave for twenty-four hours a day and for seven days a week. He had no rights, but was owned by his master in order to do his master's will. The happiness or misery of his life was dependent upon the attitude of the master. In serving Jesus Christ, the Church has a Master who, while demanding total allegiance and obedience, is gracious; and so, to serve him is not to live in fear, but in peace and joy.

In order to emphasize the great privilege which believers have in relation to God in Christ, Paul and others referred to them as sons of God or children of God. This is another image and complements rather than contradicts the image of slaves. Again, the image in each case points to the truth and is not in itself the truth. Slavery points to allegiance, while sonship points to privilege; both are important.

IMPERSONAL IMAGES

Salt of the earth. Salt has been and remains a basic commodity. It was used by primitive villagers and is still used by air travelers as they eat, flying at 37,000 feet and at 600 miles per hour. Jesus said to his disciples, "You are the salt of the earth. But if the salt loses its saltiness, how can it be made salty again? It is no longer good for anything, except to be thrown out and trampled by men" (Matthew 5:13).

Salt is essentially different in taste from the food into which it is put and is therefore able to change the taste of the whole. So the effectiveness of the Church lies in its quality and in its difference. Salt which has lost its taste is useless, and a church which has lost its Christian values and life-style and adopted those of the society in which it is found is useless in terms of extending God's kingdom.

Salt is also used to preserve meat from decay. It is still rubbed into meat in order to prevent it from going bad. So the presence of the Church in the world is to be God's agent in society, maintaining standards of honesty, faithfulness, and truthfulness in that society. Salt which has lost its power cannot preserve meat from decay, and a church which has lost its wholehearted commitment to the Lord cannot hope to set an example and affect the society in which it is found.

Light of the world. Light is one of the basic realities of our universe and easily lends itself to religious illustrations. Jesus said, "I am the light of the world. Whoever follows me will never walk in darkness, but will have the light of life" (John 8:12; cf. 9:5). Having the light of life, his disciples may be called "the light of the world." Thus in the Sermon on the Mount Jesus taught:

"You are the light of the world. A city on a hill cannot be hidden. Neither do people light a lamp and put it under a bowl. Instead they put it on its stand, and it gives light to everyone in the house. In the same way, let your light shine before men, that they may see your good deeds and praise your Father in heaven.

(Matthew 5:14-16)

For light to be effective, it needs to be placed in a strategic position—e.g., a candle in a candlestick, or a headlamp in the front of a car. A city which is built upon the crest of a hill can be seen from miles around, and a church which lives to obey God and to embody his will in action will not be missed by local residents.

Light is most appreciated when it is contrasted with darkness. So the fellowship and life-style of churches in the world is to be qualitatively different from those of the local social or political clubs. Further, light dispels darkness, and the Church has the function in the world of dispelling all those barriers which separate mankind from God and men and women from each other. Paul wrote to the Philippian church telling them to become blameless and pure and to shine as stars in the universe as they held out the word of life to a needy society (2:15).

A letter from Christ. This image occurs only once, as Paul addressed the church in Corinth:

You yourselves are our letter, written on our hearts, known and read by everybody. You show that you are a letter from Christ, the result of our ministry, written not with ink but with the Spirit of the living God, not on tablets of stone but on tablets of human hearts.

(2 Corinthians 3:2, 3)

In the context of the letter this image functions in this way: (1) The sender is Jesus Christ. (2) Its delivery is by Paul and others. (3) It is written in ink, which is the Spirit of the living God. (4) The words are inscribed on the tablets of human hearts (the Church). (5) The message is for all human beings to read. And (6) the substance of the message is a testimony to the fact that Paul is a genuine apostle of Jesus Christ. Obviously the second and sixth parts were applied to this congregation founded by Paul, but the image itself can apply to any Christian congregation.

What is important in the life of a congregation is Jesus

Christ, who is the Lord; the Holy Spirit, who is the life-giver; and people whose hearts and lives have been transformed by the gospel of Jesus through the power of the Spirit. Such a congregation is to function as a letter from Christ addressed to everyone in the neighborhood. The local population will read this letter and will see God at work in the lives of ordinary people like themselves.

MISSION

"Looking around" leads to mission and mission is a large concept. It may be claimed that everything which the Church is and does has a missionary dimension, but not everything has a missionary intention. Being in the world and being different from the world, the Church is involved in a relationship with the world. Even when there is no direct activity toward the world, there is a relationship with it. What the images of salt and light highlight is that always the Church has a missionary dimension, even when seemingly the members are involved only in worship. Light shines from a worshiping community. What the images of ambassadors and witnesses highlight is the specific activity of going into the world, or rather being sent into the world by the Lord Christ.

The mission of the Holy Trinity

The word "mission" was once used in theology only with reference to the mission of our Triune God. The Father sent the Son into the world to be the Savior of the world and Head of a new humanity; the Father and the Son sent the Spirit into the world in order to continue the work begun by the Son. In modern times mission has

been used of the going out of the Church into the world
in the name of the Triune God. Both uses are correct,
and they complement each other.

Mission begins in the love of God for the world as
displayed in the atoning death of Jesus and in his glorious resurrection and ascension. It proceeds as the Holy
Spirit continues the ministry of reconciliation in and
through the Church, founded by the Lord Jesus. The
mission of the Church is nothing less than the continuation of the mission of the Triune God and in particular
the mission of the Incarnate Son of God. So the model
for mission is Jesus himself, who told the people of his
home town:

"The Spirit of the Lord is on me,
  because he has anointed me
  to preach good news to the poor.
He has sent me to proclaim
  freedom for the prisoners
  and recovery of sight for the blind,
to release the oppressed,
  to proclaim the year of the Lord's favor."

(Luke 4:18, 19)

Here proclamation and action are intertwined.

Through the actual presence of the Church in the
world and by its distinctive worship and fellowship, mission has begun. A city built on the top of a hill cannot be
hid! It is continued as evangelism, the bringing of the
Good News to those who will hear, is done. Evangelism
is the center of the active part of mission. Evangelism is
not an "evangelistic campaign," "a revival meeting," or
"a crusade," although it may include special services. It
is a constant witnessing by the Church to the world con-

cerning what God has done and what God offers today in and through Jesus Christ, the Savior.

Embodying the message

The Church is not only the agent of evangelism, the bearer of the Good News; it is also a part of the message. The Good News is directed toward real people in concrete situations, and people and situations differ. To be meaningful, the Good News has to be presented in different ways to different people. If the Good News is taken to the lonely and the alienated, then with the proclamation and explanation will go a continuing loving care and concern by the members. If the Good News is taken to the poor and destitute, then attempts will be made to relieve the poverty and change the structures which create poverty. Good news entails good works. They belong together. So evangelism cannot be separated from social action. The Church is inseparable in practice from the Good News, for the Church witnesses by its attitude and actions as to the kind of people whom the Word and Spirit of the Lord create. Therefore, to preach and not to act, to proclaim and not to care, and to bear the Good News and not to show practical concern is not truly to evangelize in God's mission.

Obviously the mission of the Church at the local level involves every member, whatever his or her background or position. Baptism, the means of entry into the Church, is not only incorporation into the death and resurrection of Jesus Christ (Romans 6); it is also a commitment to God's mission in the world. To be baptized is to be committed to Christ, who has a continuing ministry through the Holy Spirit to the whole world. To be baptized in the name of the Father, Son, and Holy Spirit is to be involved in the mission of the Triune God.

So the Church is always involved in a double movement. It is called out of the world by the Good News and sent into the world to bear the Good News. Its life of worship and fellowship as a new community leads to mission in the world, and mission in the world strengthens its life.

Each church has to assess its own calling to mission and to execute it with reference to its own particular circumstances, which differ even in one city or geographical region. Mission in the inner city is not the same as in the suburbs. It will involve all the members, though not all will have the same task. Here the different gifts which the exalted Lord gives will come into active service, and some gifts will actually be discovered as the activity proceeds.

The whole Church in the world has a calling to mission, and this is more than the total sum of the activity of local churches. There are aspects of mission which cannot be undertaken by a local church or even a collection of local churches (e.g., a diocese). For example, the planting of churches, the creation of Christian schools and medical centers in the home country and also in foreign countries requires the resources and gifts of more than one congregation. Over the years Western churches have sent through missionary agencies some of their most dedicated and gifted members to other lands. Today some of the churches founded by this work are sending their own members to bear the Good News to other lands. We are much wiser today than we were last century to the need to preach, teach, and live in a way which makes sense in terms of local conditions and cultures. Those who still leave their home church to serve churches in other countries need to be ready to work as members of local churches and be respectful of local traditions and culture. The modern "missionary" is a slave of Jesus Christ and a servant of the churches.

Aspects of mission in debate

I recognize that the way in which the mission of the whole Church is understood in relation to the changing of social, political, and economic structures is at present in lively debate, and Christians have not reached anything like a common mind on the matter. That way of understanding mission known as "liberation theology" definitely sees the need to work for the changing of unjust structures and systems and to commit the whole Church to support of the poor and the deprived. Here the use of force is not ruled out and is by some actively encouraged. A more conservative approach recognizes the injustice existing in many parts of the world, but claims that since violence is ruled out thc Church must do all possible in a peaceful manner to alleviate the lot of the poor and to remove discrimination. Here a basic belief is that revolution is likely to replace one bad government or structure with another which is equally bad.

Then there is the relation of the Church to other religions, and the question whether salvation is found outside the Church. This also is much discussed today, and a common mind has not yet emerged. Does mission mean proclamation of the Good News followed by dialogue with committed members of other religions— e.g., Islam, Hinduism, and Buddhism? Or is dialogue a compromise of the Good News?

Obviously the meaning of mission in relation to social, political, and economic structures and to other religions needs much more careful thought in order to arrive at knowledge of the will of God. Happily, the meaning of mission in most local situations is fairly clear, and the only problem is the lack of wholehearted commitment and obedience from the church membership. In the words of Jesus, the harvest is ripe, but the reapers are few.

QUESTIONS FOR DISCUSSION

1. Is the distinction between evangelism and social action an artificial one?

2. In what sense are all Christians missionaries?

7 THE CHURCH OF CHRIST

"Jesus is Lord" was the first confession of faith in the early Church (Romans 10:9). While it remains true that for every Christian Jesus is Lord of his life, it is also true that from his ascension Jesus has been and remains the Lord of the universe (Ephesians 1:20-23; Colossians 1:15-20), the Lord of nations in history (1 Corinthians 15:24-28), and the Lord of the Church (Ephesians 4:4, 5). Having discussed in Chapter Two the general relationship of God and the Church, I want here to consider the specific relationship of Jesus, the Messiah and exalted Lord, to the Church, whose salvation he purchased by his precious blood (1 Peter 1:19). Doing this task will entail examining the image of "the body," which appears to have been one of Paul's favorite images of the Church, and also the meaning of "the head [of the body]."

THE HEAD

The Greek word which is translated as "head" is *kephale.* Many people seem to think that when Paul spoke of the head and the body, he was thinking of the whole human body from head to toe and presenting the church as that which is below the neck and Christ as that which is above the neck. Such thinking is misguided. Paul was presenting "the head" and "the body" as two separate images which he ran alongside each other.

Writing to the church in Colossae, Paul taught that "in Christ all the fullness of the Deity lives in bodily form, and you have been given fullness in Christ, who is the head over every power and authority" (2:9, 10). Paul held that the Son of God, who is our Savior, is the ruler over all powers in the universe. Writing to the church in Ephesus, he made the further claim that "God placed all things under his feet and appointed him to be head over everything for the church, which is his body, the fullness of him who fills everything in every way" (1:22, 23).

Not only does the headship of Christ mean that he rules the universe and the Church; it also means that he sustains them, keeping them operating according to the will of the Father. Paul taught that Christ "is before all things, and in him all things hold together" (Colossians 1:17) and from Christ "the whole body, joined and held together by every supporting ligament, grows and builds itself up in love, as each part does its work" (Ephesians 4:16; cf. Colossians 2:19). As the "beginning" or "archetype," he is the One through whom and for whom the Church was planned by the Father (Colossians 1:18, 19). As the "firstborn from among the dead," he is the head of a people who have died and been raised with him (Colossians 1:18; 2:12, 20).

So we see that to speak of Christ the Head is to say much more than that he is the ruler of the Church. It is also to confess that he is the giver of all that is needed by his people for growth in grace, knowledge, and holy living.

In Ephesians 4:7ff. Paul presented the exalted Lord
Jesus, conqueror of all his enemies, as the sole giver of
good gifts to the Church. He had in mind gifts of ministry and declared that Christ's purpose in giving these
gifts of preachers, teachers, and pastors is "to prepare
God's people for works of service, so that the body of
Christ may be built up until we all reach unity in the
faith and in the knowledge of the Son of God and become mature, attaining to the whole measure of the
fullness of Christ" (vv. 12, 13). Some gifts, apostles for
example, were given by the exalted, triumphant Lord to
the whole Church while others, pastors for example,
were and are given to individual churches. Whether the
gifts be for the universal or the local situation, their
function is to bring harmony, wholeness, unity, love,
and maturity to the churches. Paul urged the Ephesians
to "make every effort to keep the unity of the Spirit
through the bond of peace" (4:3). Also, he called upon
the Colossians to "let the peace of Christ rule in your
hearts, since as members of one body you were called to
peace" (3:15).

THE BODY

The image of the body was used by Paul of the whole
Church (Colossians 1:18) and of the local church (Colossians 3:15). In the letters to the churches in Rome and
Corinth he freely used the image of the body in order to
emphasize in those congregations both dependence on
Christ in the power of the Spirit and the interdependence of the members. In Romans 12:3-8 Paul was emphasizing the need for humility in the Church, which
meant that all should recognize what spiritual gifts
Christ had given to each of the members. "Just as each
of us has one body with many members, and these

members do not all have the same function, so in Christ we who are many form one body, and each member belongs to all the others" (vv. 4, 5). Different members had such gifts as prophesying, serving, teaching, encouraging, contributing to the needs of others, leadership, and showing mercy.

In 1 Corinthians 12:12-30 Paul provided a full development of the image of the body. Earlier he had used the word "body" in three related ways—in order to emphasize the need for purity of life (6:13-15), the repudiation of idolatry (10:14-17), and the serious commitment involved in partaking of the Lord's Supper (11:27-29). These three usages lead on to the image of the Church as the body of Christ, but before he came to this image he listed various gifts of the Spirit possessed by individual members at Corinth. They were the message of wisdom, the message of knowledge, special faith, healing, miraculous powers, prophecy, distinguishing between spirits, speaking in different tongues, and the interpretation of tongues (12:8-11). The image of the body was used to teach the church that its members belong one to another, because they all belong to the Lord and because they are nourished by the Spirit of the Lord.

The body is a unit, though it is made up of many parts; and though all its parts are many, they form one body. So it is with Christ. For we were all baptized by one Spirit into one body—whether Jews or Greeks, slave or free—and we were all given the one Spirit to drink.

(12:12-14)

Following the explanation of the image of the body, he made a further list of gifts of the Spirit—apostles, prophets, teachers, workers of miracles, healing, helping others, administration, and speaking in different tongues. Then he set his whole discussion in a large context, the context of love, which is presented as that which makes the "body" function in a healthy way, as if it were the bloodstream and the nervous system.

IMPLICATIONS FOR TODAY

The widespread use of this image in churches today, often to the neglect of other images, is eloquent testimony to the fact that it "speaks" to persons who live in modern Western society. Here I wish to make various comments on the use and meaning of the image.

1. To speak of the Church as "the body" is to use an image or picture which highlights a truth or several truths. Many seem to use this image as though it were the equivalent of a proposition such as "believers belong to Christ." This leads to confusion of thought!

2. What this image primarily highlights when it stands alone is the interdependence of the members of the Church. They need each other, and they need the gifts which Christ gives to each one through the ministry of the Holy Spirit. Experience reveals that interdependence is not easily achieved in a church made up of typical Western Christians. Not only our pride, but also the accumulated presuppositions and habits of a lifetime have to be removed. To work toward interdependence is both a costly and an enriching experience. I give myself to others—that is costly; they give themselves to me—that is enriching.

3. What the image of Christ as "head" of "the body" highlights has three parts. First, the Church local and universal owes primary allegiance to Christ as its Ruler, King, Lord, and Savior. His word, his law, his way, and his standards cannot be changed to meet the whims and fancies of men and women. The Lord Jesus Christ rules

through his Word, which should be faithfully preached, taught, and explained in order to be believed and obeyed.

Secondly, the Church local and universal is sustained in grace, love, and power by the Lord Jesus through the work of the Holy Spirit. Only by this spiritual and moral power can the people of God grow together toward maturity. The pursuit of personal holiness is fine, but the Church also needs to grow in corporate holiness.

Thirdly, the ministry of the Church to each member and to the needy world is the work of Christ, for it is the continuation of the work he began in Galilee, Judea, and Samaria. He who is "head" of the Church is also Lord of the universe, of history, and of nations; and in the world he is represented by his "body," the Church.

4. The close association of the images of "head" and "body" provided for Paul what amounted to an explosive truth in the social world of both Judaism and the Roman Empire. This truth shattered all contemporary views of social organization, removing racialisms, nationalisms, and particularisms. Members of the body of Christ had been liberated by their Head from all those powers which caused divisions in human society and had been given the spiritual power to be a society in which "there is no Greek or Jew, circumcised or uncircumcised, barbarian, Scythian, slave or free" (Colossians 3:11). To the Ephesians, Paul spoke of "one new man" (as we noted in Chapter Five) and also of reconciling Jew and Gentile in "one body." Human nature has changed little, if at all, since Paul's day, and churches today are still called in the power of the Spirit to produce this type of society where there is total reconciliation between members from different backgrounds.

5. Finally, the place of gifts in the local church needs

careful thought in order to benefit from the provision of the Holy Spirit from Christ, the Head. Those who are ordained to be pastors and bishops, as well as those who officially preach, teach, and serve, should be those to whom the exalted Lord has given appropriate gifts which have been recognized by the Church. But this by no means exhausts the existence and use of gifts. It is the duty of a church to discover which gifts exist or are latent within the membership and to encourage them. Where the more spectacular gifts exist—e.g., speaking in different tongues—their use in worship and fellowship will, as Paul taught, be carefully controlled. Gifts exist to edify the membership and to enable it to be involved in God's mission to the world.

QUESTIONS FOR DISCUSSION

1. What is it in the image of the body which has made it so attractive to many Christians in recent times?

2. "Interdependence is only painfully learned by a church in Western society because self-sufficiency is widely encouraged as a virtue." Is this true or false? Give your reasons.

8 CONCLUSION

Our study of the biblical images of the Church is now complete and a summary of the argument is needed. The basic truth to which most, if not all, of the images point is that the essence (true nature) and form (existence in time and space) of the Church cannot be separated. The imperfect and misguided church in Corinth was "God's building." To claim that essence and form are inseparable is not to claim that one form is as good as another. There is a minimum form and a maximum form. Because of our sinfulness, no church ever reaches or expresses the maximum and we have to wait for the age to come to see this maximum. The minimum is not easy to define, for in the last analysis only God knows whether a congregation is his church. A common Protestant answer has been to say that where the Word is faithfully preached and the sacraments of the Lord's Supper and baptism rightly administered, there is the Church. Of course, no church should be content with a minimum form, but should be striving in grace toward the maximum.

Based on the model of the Church being a congregation which looks back to its brethren and sisters in history, up to God, forward to the glorious age to come, and around to a sinful and needy world, and remembering that Jesus is Lord (Head) of the Church, it has been argued that in the form of the Church should be the following ingredients:

1. The recognition of the historical continuity of the people of God and the use of means of this recognition—e.g., liturgy, succession of ordained ministers, orthodox doctrine, infant baptism, etc.

2. The centrality of corporate worship on the Lord's Day, with the Eucharist as the focal point.

3. The development of a life style and an attitude to fellowship, ownership of property, and involvement in secular society which reflects the pilgrim status of the Church on earth.

4. The practice of mission, involving what we are as well as what we do and say.

5. The cultivation of fellowship in the congregation which reflects the reconciliation achieved for us by Christ and the use of all the gifts he gives through the Spirit.

It has been recognized that no church wholly contains these ingredients.

So the question arises as to whether these five ingredients can be placed in any kind of order of priority. I think that they can be, as long as it is recognized that I am answering the question, Which church should I join? My order is 1 followed by 2, and then 3, 4, 5 may come in any order, for they tend to promote each other.

The justification which I offer is quite simple. While an independent church may have an excellent preacher and/or pastor, be involved in mission, and enjoy good fellowship, it can never gain the historical dimension of continuity. Of necessity, in an independent church this must be absent. On the other hand, my 3, 4 and 5 can be cultivated in any congregation of committed Christians. Thus, I would look for a congregation which has deep historical roots and which, by the grace of God, has the potential to begin to express the full form of God's Church. This means I have to join one of the "traditional" denominations. I personally chose the Anglican or Episcopalian Church because it seemed to me to be able, more easily than other churches I know, to become what the Church is intended to be by the Lord Jesus Christ. I accept that others, in search of what I was in search of, have joined the Roman Catholic, Orthodox, Lutheran, and Presbyterian Churches.

In concluding, I need to make two further points. The first is that I have not been saying that members of congregationally governed or other types of churches are not true Christians. And I have not been saying that such churches do not possess the essence of the Church. Rather, I have argued that their form does not truly reflect the essence. If an army general dressed as a major or an admiral dressed as a commander, neither man would do justice to the truth. God's Church ought to have the best form.

The second is that while I think that the large Roman Catholic Church and Greek Orthodox Church are true churches, I also think that in certain of their doctrines and dogmas they are in error. Certainly, on the fundamental doctrines of the Holy Trinity and the Person and work of Christ they hold to pure orthodoxy. Further, they have maintained historical continuity in a quite remarkable way over the centuries. Yet in aspects of their doctrines about the Virgin Mary and in some of the forms of veneration offered to her and other saints they go beyond the clear teaching of Scripture. Thus, we pray for the continuing renewal and reform of these churches. Great changes have come into the Roman Catholic Church since the Second Vatican Council, and what the Lord plans to do in the future we cannot tell. And Protestants must be careful in their criticisms, for their own house needs to be put in order in so many ways. At the bar of Holy Scripture all churches, even those we may think are scripturally pure, are pronounced lacking in one or other aspect of that which makes up the true form of the Church.

QUESTIONS FOR DISCUSSION

1. Do historical roots really matter? If so, why?

2. What must happen for a Church which can trace its existence back to primitive times to cease to be God's Church? (Perhaps the history of the people of Israel, God's covenantal community, will throw some light on this question.)

APPENDIX
The Ordained Ministry

I add this appendix especially for two types of people who I find are fairly common today among Christians. First, those who in their thinking about the Church want help in forming a doctrine of the place and function of the men whom we call pastors, priests, ministers of religion, and bishops. Secondly, those who "feel a call to ministry" and are thinking of going to a theological college/seminary. (Americans speak of seminaries and Britishers of colleges!)

GIFTS AND MINISTRY

Every church member has a ministry. The exalted Lord gives to each a gift and the exercise of this gift in or for the Church's ministry. This is certainly one of the truths highlighted by Paul's image of the Church as a body. Certain gifts tend to give prominence to those who possess them; for example, the gift of prophesying or exhorting must be exercised publicly. Other gifts can be exercised unobtrusively—for example, the gift of caring for and communicating with the elderly, sick, and shut-ins. The Church may be described as a fellowship of gifts of the Spirit. So Peter could write: "Each one should use whatever gift he has received to serve others, faithfully administering God's grace in its various forms" (1 Peter 4:10).

Not only was the emphasis on service prominent in the teaching of Jesus. He also provided the model for all Christian service. Here are several of his significant sayings:

"If anyone wants to be first, he must be the very last, and the servant of all."

(Mark 9:35)

"Whoever wants to become great among you must be your servant, and whoever wants to be first must be slave of all."

(Mark 10:43, 44)

"The greatest among you will be your servant. For whoever exalts himself will be humbled, and whoever humbles himself will be exalted."

(Matthew 23:11, 12)

Just before the Feast of the Passover, when he died on the cross as the sacrificial Lamb for our sins, Jesus washed his disciples' feet, which was the task of the household servant. After doing this menial job, he gave some teaching on service: "I tell you the truth, no servant is greater than his master, nor is a messenger greater than the one who sent him" (John 13:16). The model Jesus chose for himself from the Old Testament was that of the Suffering Servant of the LORD (Isaiah 52:13—53:12), and the model which is given us by God is Jesus, the Servant of the LORD.

THE ORDAINED MINISTRY

Those whom we call clergy, ministers of religion, parish priests, bishops, and pastors should be those to whom the exalted Lord has given gifts which the people of God have recognized as being suitable for holding "office" in the churches. This recognition has led to what we call ordination—the formal setting apart with prayer and laying on of hands—to the ministry of leadership, preaching, teaching, and administration of the sacraments. This ministry is usually but not necessarily a full-time task. Most of what a clergyman does can be done by others, especially in a church where all the members are exercising their gifts. In such situations, he will support, encourage, and inspire further service and worship of the Lord. A focal point of leadership is necessary and that leader or that group of leaders should, like their Master, give the example of true service. The church does not belong to the pastor or parish priest or bishop; rather, he is a member of it who by the consent of all exercises his gifts in leading this people.

On this basis, I want to portray the ordained minister as a godly and learned man. In presenting this, I am presuming that he is a "professional" in the sense that he knows how to read well in public, how to lead services of worship with reverence and dignity, how to compose prayers for public use, how to conduct weddings, funerals, etc., and how to preach. There is no excuse for slovenliness or sloppiness in the conducting of worship.

Learned. When I say "learned," I mean that his understanding is developed as far as his ability and intelligence allow. Also, I mean that the learning will be that which belongs to the calling of a pastor in the Church of God. As a minimum, he must understand the Scriptures, the "tradition" of the Church, and the human situation in which the church he serves is placed and operates.

Learning in the Scriptures is gained and increased by

a regular, disciplined study of the books of the Bible. There will be careful exegesis of each paragraph of each book and then a synthesis of the fruits of exegesis to produce a biblical theology, the teaching of God on particular practical aspects of our pilgrimage. This continuing work should occupy the pastor for the whole of his life. This is the primary source of food for his soul. Then there will be further detailed exegesis in order to prepare specific talks and sermons. In both these endeavors use will be made of such aids as lexicons, dictionaries, and commentaries. Those who listen to such a man will know that his thoughts are constantly being refreshed and extended.

Learning in the tradition of the Church will enable the pastor to know what the people of God before him taught as the Faith, to understand the practice of spirituality and the offering of worship to God. He will learn of their successes and their failures, their insights and their errors and this learning will extend his understanding of the calling of the church which he serves. So a pastor cannot neglect the study of Church history.

Learning in terms of understanding the local situation, its culture, and its ethos will enable the pastor the more effectively to communicate with and to bring Christ to the people of God he leads and the society in which they live. We all know that while there is in Western society a common layer of culture, areas even in one city differ considerably. The people who live in suburbia and the people who live in the inner city are not usually the same types, but both need the gospel. To understand people in the society in which they live is a hard task, but it is a task for the pastor to undertake.

This learning will necessarily make a man wiser. However, as a servant of Jesus Christ the increase in wisdom will be for the benefit of the people of God. It will thus be a God-centered learning and will develop as he grows in grace and obedience.

I recognize that saying all this is easy, but practicing it is difficult. Yet it needs to be said and to be said forcibly in love. I have bought for theological institutions many libraries of clergy, and what I have seen has surprised me. Most British clergy appear to buy very few serious theological books—commentaries, liturgical, devotional, and theological studies—after they leave college/ seminary. Publishers tell me that ministers of religion are poor buyers of serious theological literature. If the reason for this seeming lack of serious reading is only financial, then steps could be taken to remedy the situation. I suspect, however, that it relates more to motivation and discipline. Summer schools, refresher courses, and the like are useful, but the committed pastor cannot neglect the pursuit of learning for the glory of God and benefit of his calling. It is the duty of the members of the church to encourage the pastor to pursue learning.

Godly. When I say "godly," I mean living in spiritual communion with God and having the mind of Jesus Christ. The Church was chosen by God the Father, redeemed by the Son, and sanctified by the Holy Spirit (1 Peter 1:2). To serve the people of God is to share in God's work. Thus, communion with God is necessary in order to participate in his love and concern for his people. Of course, every Christian is called to perfection and wholeness (Matthew 5:48; 1 Peter 1:16). But in the case of the pastor, it is crucial that his life be God-centered so that he sets the right example to those who look to him and to those who expect care from him.

The New Testament contains much teaching and many exhortations on this theme. Jesus used the picture of the vine with its branches to teach the disciples that they needed to be constantly united to him in faith and love, for without him they could do nothing (John 15:4ff.). Paul told his assistant Timothy "to flee from all (immorality and love of money) and pursue righteousness, godliness, faith, love, endurance and gentleness" (1 Timothy 6:11ff.). In the same letter, he set out the qualities for which he looked in those to be appointed as leaders in the local church (3:1-13). To summarize them, it may be said that they point to practical godliness.

It may be claimed that to survive as a pastor and to carry the burdens of the flock, godliness is needed. To be involved wholly in mission to the world, godliness is needed. To worship God in spirit and in truth, godliness is needed.

Godliness is a gift of God. However, he usually gives it in small portions over a long period of time as the believer submits to and cooperates with the divine will. In order to grow in grace and cultivate the mind of Christ, it is surely necessary to set apart time each day for meditation and prayer. Study to be learned for Christ's sake may well lead on to meditation and prayer, but the latter should not be neglected. A full-time pastor is privileged in that he can order his life so as to set apart time daily for meditation and prayer. He needs to be cut off from the demands of telephone and family and congregation in order to be alone with the Lord. Only as the pastor finds time for this cultivation of communion with God will his vision be renewed and extended and his love deepened and enriched. Judged by the standards of Christ, a pastor who neglects the pursuit of godliness will never be successful. He may be an excellent administrator, a fine preacher, and a delightful personality, but without godliness he will not lead the people of God nearer to God. Church members should pray for their pastor and encourage him to find time to meet daily with his Lord.

The place of theological colleges/seminaries. It has become the general rule that those who are called by God to be pastors go to an institution in order to prepare for this service. Ideally such an institution should have at least the following characteristics:

1. *It should be a worshiping community.* Daily corporate worship should be the structure and should set the tone of all study of Scripture, tradition, history, and culture. Theology not pursued in the context of worship can so easily become merely academic and cerebral.

2. *It should be a community which, given its peculiar circumstances, attempts to live as a community of Christians.* To use the biblical image, it should attempt to be "the body of Christ." Preparation for ministry involves learning to love and appreciate others who are brothers and sisters in Christ.

3. *It should receive as a sacred trust the Scriptures and the tradition of the Church handed down with the Scriptures in the life of the historical Church.* The study of theology should be pursued as an activity of the ongoing people of God, and theologians should always remember that they are servants of Christ and his Church.

4. *It should attempt to live and to think the Christian faith in ways which are meaningful for its own time and culture.* Armed with the thoughts of the centuries, it will cross the frontier to the modern world speaking and developing a life-style which is relevant and meaningful for people who live in an increasingly technological society. So the tensions and problems of faith will be acutely felt and answers will be attempted.

5. *It should attempt to develop the gift(s) which each person possesses and also to teach suitable professional skills.* A foundation should be laid on which a life of ministry can be built.

I recognize that the ideal is rarely within our reach. Today our problems are complicated in both North America and Europe by the growing number of married men who study theology; this makes community life and worship more difficult to arrange. Further, the massive size of some seminaries in the U.S.A. appears to make corporate worship and community life impossible. My own view is that a college/seminary should not exceed 200 students, for while academic resources may be increased by going over that number, what is lost in terms of the corporate life is too precious to lose.

The theological college/seminary cannot give a call to a person to be a pastor. It exists to serve the Church by cultivating, refining, and developing the gifts which God has given naturally and which the exalted Lord has given specifically to those whom the people of God believe should be pastors.

QUESTIONS FOR DISCUSSION

1. What purpose, if any, does the ordained minister have in the church?

2. Are theological colleges/seminaries doing the best job that they could do?

FURTHER READING

POPULAR LEVEL

1. Bloesch, Donald and Webber, Robert, eds. *The Orthodox Evangelicals: Who They Are and What They Are Saying.* Nashville: Thomas Nelson, Inc., 1978. This symposium was written by men who attended the Chicago Call in May 1977 and has several very helpful essays—e.g., on the sacraments by Tom Howard.

2. Toon, Peter. *Jesus Christ Is Lord.* London: Marshall, Morgan and Scott; Valley Forge, Pa.: Judson Press, 1978. This is a theology of the ascension and examines the meaning of the Lordship of Christ over the Church, universe, and history.

3. Watson, David. *I Believe in the Church.* London: Hodder and Stoughton; Grand Rapids: Wm. B. Eerdmans, 1978. This is useful, for its author is a successful evangelist and pastor and he writes from this rich experience.

A MORE ADVANCED LEVEL

1. Berkouwer, G. C. *The Church.* Grand Rapids: Wm. B. Eerdmans, 1978. This is a solid, perceptive study by a

leading Reformed (Presbyterian) theologian, examining the meaning of "one, holy, catholic and apostolic."

2. Bosch, David. *Witness to the World: A Theology of Mission.* London: Marshall, Morgan and Scott; Atlanta: John Knox Press, 1980. This is the best book I know on this topic.

3. Küng, Hans. *The Church.* London: Search Press; Garden City, N.Y.: Image, 1968. This is a brilliant book and I warmly commend it.

4. Minear, Paul S. *Images of the Church in the New Testament.* Philadelphia: Westminster Press, 1960. This is a systematic study of ninety-six images.

5. Toon, Peter. *The Development of Doctrine in the Church.* Cambridge: James Clarke Ltd.; Grand Rapids: Wm. B. Eerdmans, 1979. This deals with the problem of the continuity of doctrine in the Church over the centuries.